FROM THE INSIDE

40 years of reflections on government, politics and events in the Utica-Rome area

By Rodger Potocki

To Vicki & John,
To two great people &
good friends

INFI∞ITY
PUBLISHING

Copyright © 2010 by Rodger Potocki

Cover photo: Utica City Hall in the 1960s, before the wrecking ball, courtesy of the Oneida County Historical Society website, www.oneidacountyhistory.org.

ISBN 0-7414-6155-2

Printed in the United States of America

Published September 2010

INFINITY PUBLISHING
1094 New DeHaven Street, Suite 100
West Conshohocken, PA 19428-2713
Toll-free (877) BUY BOOK
Local Phone (610) 941-9999
Fax (610) 941-9959
Info@buybooksontheweb.com
www.buybooksontheweb.com

For Fred Nassar, the best and brightest who left us too soon.

Table of Contents

Preface

With age, one tends to reflect more on the past than the future. I have been in and around politics and politicians in the Utica-Rome area for almost 45 years. During most of that period, I have been privy to an insider's view of political leaders, how they governed and how some very important public issues were decided. And these activities allowed me to meet, know and assess a pretty impressive array of state and national politicians.

I concluded that my experiences should become part of recorded local history. History has played an important part of my life since my college days. I was very fortunate to be exposed to such professors as Bill Askew at Colgate University and Harry Jackson, and Bob Anderson at Utica College of Syracuse University. They whetted my appetite for both history and public service. The graduate school I attended specialized in government in theory and practice. In the 1960's, public service was considered among the noblest of callings by those my age. Being born and raised in Utica, NY, added to the attraction. Utica and the greater Utica area was one of the most fascinating and colorful political models one could find. The Utica-Rome area has been characterized by incorrigible political characters, important political relationships and defining issues that not only warrant recording but provide an interesting and educational insight into government and politics. This early exposure to history and political thought led to most of my adult career and to the decision to now share some of it.

I am one of few in the area who can contribute to the historical record from a rather unique, "behind the closed door" perspective. Let's face it; the average person has little knowledge of how his political representatives act and make decisions prior to those decisions being made public. And, often unseen events play the dominant role in political decision making. It is my hope that the sharing of my privileged perspective will assist in the understanding of how and why aspects of our area's history unfolded as they did. It is also my wish that that understanding of the past will contribute to a better future for the area I call home.

I was fortunate to meet one of the smartest people I've ever known, Fred Nassar, at an early age. Fred inspired me to think about the role of politics and political leadership in the development of a community. He viewed politics as an art and political leaders as the artists. The artist produces bad art, mediocre art, memorable art, great art. Our communities reflect the artists who paint them. They rise, they fall, they grow, and they contract in a large part due to the leadership they produce.

People select leaders and leaders drive public sector issues and solutions. In our democratic system, those we elect reflect who we are and what we aspire to be. The mosaic presented in this book of recollections adds to the story of how we came to be what we are today as an area from 1965 to the present. It is limited to the direct, personal experiences I had as an "insider" in an area I have called home since birth. It also provides some entertaining glimpses of people and situations that reflected the interesting character of the area. If nothing else, it cannot be denied that the Utica-Rome area has an interesting and entertaining past and cast. That part of our history and culture should be forever remembered.

Finally, I hope that the book can accomplish more than providing a chronology of people and events, by piquing the interest of today's young people who are attracted to local government and politics. In our area, our best and brightest have not been sufficiently encouraged to assist in defining the community in which they live. My goal is that this book will not only record history but help inspire others to help bring about political and civic change that will contribute to a more positive and brighter future to a place we call home.

Rodger Potocki

Prologue

In late spring of 1965, I was one of a group playing a round of golf at Valley View Golf Course, the fine tract owned by the City of Utica. I recall saying to my friend Sam Vedete that it would be fun to get involved in local politics that summer. It was a mayoral election year and I had read of a reform Republican candidate named Dominick Assaro, who was challenging the incumbent mayor, Frank Dulan, in a primary. Assaro was building a campaign based on keeping and attracting young adults in and to Utica. That theme piqued our interest.

Sam and I were seniors at Utica College and were heading off to graduate school in the fall. We had known each other since the 8th grade but had taken different paths to high school and college. Sam was a Catholic school kid and I, a public school one. He went to Utica Catholic Academy and I, to Utica Free Academy for our high school educations. I was a jock and he wasn't which meant our paths crossed infrequently in those years. But we did, as they say, see each other around. A friendship was understood.

I had made my way to Utica College via Colgate University. I went to Colgate for two basic reasons, to play basketball and baseball and because it was close to home. The close to home part was important because I was madly in love with my high school girlfriend who was a year behind me in school and age. Being a scant 30 miles away allowed me to run home nearly every weekend. That led to a not too uncommon occurrence in the 1950s and early 1960s—an early marriage.

In those days, Colgate had a policy that undergraduates getting married were asked to withdraw from school for one year and would receive automatic re-admittance after the year. The university wanted students to get their marriage started away from college life and all of its demands, pressures and potential pitfalls.

I had gotten married during the first part of my second semester. I hid the fact from the college, not wanting to be asked to leave immediately. I told only my roommates and my DKE fraternity brothers. A little flavor of the times was apparent when my marriage was discussed at a DKE gathering in the house. The president made the announcement and then asked all married brothers to stand. About a quarter stood. I was stunned. They were all secret to me up to that point. In those days, abortions were not an option to most for various reasons. The standard was to get married and become responsible for one's actions.

I decided to quietly transfer to Utica College of Syracuse University for the following year. I made arrangements for a basketball scholarship through Tom Huggins, the athletic director. Utica College would also mean that my wife and I would remain in close proximity to our parents who could provide us with needed support. College would also be less costly and I could work as I was educated.

Sam arrived at Utica College the conventional way. When I transferred in, we immediately became good friends. We were both Social Studies majors and, shared classes. We were politically conservative. At UC, I carried a full time course load and worked 40 hours a week, afternoons and evenings. My new wife and I rented a third floor walk up and soon were joined by our baby boy. We were to continue developing a family. In a life of family, school, sports and work, there was not a wasted or dull moment.

As juniors in 1964, Sam, along with another friend, Bob Hubble, and I decided to form a college Young Republicans Club. We were really inspired by Barry Goldwater's presidential campaign. Others joined and our ranks swelled to about ten or eleven, counting girlfriends! Even then it was hard to find a conservative on a college campus.

We started dueling on campus with our Democratic counterparts and also tried to generate some media attention. We contacted local Republican Party officials and convinced them that we had hordes of young volunteers available for duty to the cause. They bought into the exaggeration and we were given local roles in both the Presidential campaign and that of U.S. Senator Ken Keating from New York. Bobby Kennedy, who had become a New Yorker, was challenging the Republican incumbent. As Senator, Keating was a popular moderate Republican, liked and respected by New Yorkers of all stripes. Kennedy was running on the strength of his name and rightly sensed that the Presidential matchup would sweep him in.

Democrats, including those on campus, were very defensive about Kennedy's campaign. They fought to limit debate on the senatorial election and only emphasized the Goldwater/Johnson conflict. But after all, that was the Presidential race, the big enchilada.

The local Republicans were happy to have our clubs help in both races. We did a good job of inflating our numbers by churning out work assigned to us. I'll never forget the time the party sent boxes of Goldwater campaign literature to my apartment for our volunteers to distribute house to house. They covered the stairway from the first floor to the third! You couldn't get in or out. What a mess. We were caught. Not quite. A few of us loaded the boxes in our cars and under the cover of darkness, dumped the lot into the Barge Canal. We did make a show of working in various neighborhoods with the few bodies we did have. I have no idea if we fooled anyone or not. In any event, we had fun and even got to meet the 1964 Republican Vice Presidential candidate, Bill Miller when he had a rally in Utica. Our first foray into real politics was a profound failure when the Goldwater ticket took the worst drubbing in American presidential election history.

But, we were bitten with the political bug. We became committed to politics and political action. To us, it was both noble and exciting. That led to the golf course conversation. We craved the local political action and Assaro seemed to fit our interests. I told Sam that I would check the candidate out and let him know if Assaro would be a good guy to whom we could offer our support.

That golf course talk, and the decision to get involved in local politics, were to determine the course of my life and ultimately, to the writing of this book.

Chapter One

The Assaro Years—1965-1971

In the spring of 1965, Utica was a robust city with a population of a little over 110,000. As the seat of Oneida County government, it was part of a metropolitan area of some 350,000, located in central New York State. The city's economy had by then transitioned from one as a knitting mill center, to one dominated by large manufacturers such as General Electric, Bendix, Sperry Rand, Chicago Pneumatic and a host of smaller, robust industries. The industrial connection to the defense industry was strong. The area's largest employer was the huge, sprawling Grifffiss Air Force Base, located in Rome, 20 miles to the northeast. The Base employed over 10,000.The area's economy was rocked in the early 1960s when part of the Air Base, the Rome Air Material Administration (ROAMA) was relocated to Oklahoma, causing the loss of several thousand jobs and residents. That move, prompted by Washington politics, not strategic defense or cost issues, was an eye opener for many in the Utica area, including a man named Fred Nassar.

In 1965, Nassar was the 42 year-old Chief Counsel of Procurement at Griffiss AFB. Fred, a Utica resident, was a Syracuse University graduate with a Harvard Law degree. He was both brilliant and dedicated to the community of his birth. Nassar understood a couple of basic facts of economic and political life in the area. First, the ROAMA loss demonstrated the importance of the base to the area's economy. Second, it showed how susceptible the base was to political pirating. Political power in Congress was shifting from the Northeast to the South and West, largely due to southerners holding long term committee chairmanships. Committee chairmen in turn, could reward their own districts, regions and states with government installations.

The overreliance on the Base, in Nassar's mind, meant both needing to build a stronger political punch to guard against future mission poaching and to diversify the area's industrial base.

Nassar thought that there was tremendous potential to grow his home area through the synergy between the scientific intelligence mission at the base, the then Rome Air Defense Center (now Rome Labs) and local industry. Technology, or tech transfer wasn't a term in those days, but that's exactly what he grasped; that local industry could be grown through government contracts and, perhaps more significant, private industry could be spun off from RADC. Two things were essential to realizing the Nassar development goal. First and foremost, protect the base and its missions. Second, grow the area's high tech educational framework which could feed both RADC and local industry. The vehicle Fred envisioned for the latter was to locate a State University of New York (SUNY) that offered engineering degrees in the Utica area. It was clear to him and others that politics on both the national and state levels would determine whether or not both goals succeeded.

It was also felt by Fred and many with whom he interacted that Utica's image as being corrupt was hurting its capacity to compete both politically and economically with other areas. This corruption was also a hindrance to attracting qualified, dedicated people to the civic arena. This thinking formed the foundation of what became the Assaro movement.

The Assaro movement was an effort to seize political control of the City of Utica and to use that control to elevate the city to a new level of growth and prosperity. To fully understand its development, a brief primer on the politics of the day will be helpful.

For decades, during and after WWII, Utica was a city of classic boss politics. The boss was Rufus Elefante, an Italian immigrant who, once here, quickly understood the rewards of politics and political control. Elefante, in concert with a small group of wealthy businessmen, ultimately built a powerful political machine that had a grasp on most aspects of daily life in and around the city. To this day, many claim that Rufie was a positive force for Utica. There is some merit to this claim, particularly from an economic point of view. Elefante and those behind him built a powerful machine that did reach state and national movers and shakers, particularly during and right after the World War II period. That influence helped determine the location and construction of Griffiss Air Force Base in Rome. Many defense oriented manufacturers mentioned followed. But, part of the Elefante equation was crime and political corruption. This grew with time and increased power. The Elefante experience was classic to other areas of boss politics in America during that period and to tendencies of virtual dictatorships of any stripe to become corrupt and all consuming.

A story of my own experience in the Elefante era, gives a small glimpse of the atmosphere. My father was a bit player in the political machine for a period of time. He was a foot soldier of Rufie's West Utica boss, Dennis O'Dowd. Uncle Denny, as he was called, oversaw the politics, patronage, houses of prostitution and gaming in West Utica under Elefante. In 1958, my dad took his young, teenage son to see Uncle Denny to land a summer job. At that time, O'Dowd was the head of the City of Utica Board of Water Supply. When we entered his office, Uncle Denny was sitting behind a huge desk. He stood up and walked to me and started to circle me, giving me the up and down. When he finished, he said that he was, "just trying to measure you to see how long a shovel you'd need."That meant I was hired. We left with a thank you and a strong handshake.

The Monday after school ended, I started work at, "the yard," located on Kemble Street in the Cornhill section of the city. My mother outfitted me in work boots and bought me my first lunch pail. That year, 1958, was not an election year, so summer hiring was sparse. The system at the yard was that all employees would gather outside first thing in the morning, and crew bosses would put together their crews. All of the regular employees were on a particular crew and members were only shared and shifted around to meet emergency needs. I was the only high school kid hired that year along with several college kids. The first morning I was not called to work on a crew. A couple of others weren't either. To make a long story short, we were never called. For weeks, I passed the time reading, sleeping in the rag bin, washing the cars of older workers and sweeping up. It was so boring that daily, I prayed for rain. That's because on rainy days, everyone stayed in and huge poker games were held. I lost my first two weeks' pay playing, and quickly learned poker the hard way.

After weeks of doing nothing of real work, an old Irishman named Pete Burns, in his Irish brogue, asked me to take a walk with him. We walked to the back of the yard. He looked at me and said, "Kid, are you stupid? Haven't you figured out by now that you don't have to be here?" I asked him what he meant. He said that I was Uncle Denny's boy and the word was not to work me. He told me to punch in every morning, be present at the crew round up, wait a half hour after everyone left and then hop the back fence and go home or do whatever I wanted. He said that someone would punch me out. I later learned that wasn't even necessary since it was Uncle Denny's guy from downtown HQ who gathered the time cards and figured out the payroll. I also learned that everyone who had a full time job had to kick back a bit of his salary every two weeks to, support the Party. This was Rufie's tribute. So, here I was as a young teenager, learning about a padded payroll and political kick-backs. Some lesson in government.

It is important to understand that during the Elefante days, there was no two party political system in the area. Rufie ran Utica. Oneida County government was run under a Board of Supervisors, led by Harold Kirch of Camden. The understanding between Elefante and Kirch was, you take yours, I take mine, and we leave each other alone. It was détente that was based on maintaining the political status quo and control. Readers of today should also understand that the area was very urban, with Utica being the large, dominant city. At the time, suburbs like New Hartford and Whitesboro were still primarily farm areas. In high school sports, we Utica Free Academy kids used to joke about playing, the Whitesboro farmers. Utica was the big prize of political riches in more ways than one. Rufie was the big power controlling jobs, money and more while the Republicans had Rome and the small rural areas. Rufie's influence overshadowed the entire area.

By the late 1950s, political reform was in the air. Two events transpired that were to cause major political change. The first was by far the most important. That was the decision by Governor Averell Harriman in 1958, to appoint a special commission to investigate crime and political corruption in Utica. Things had gotten so far out of hand that even a Democratic governor saw the need to step in. The Fisher Commission, named after Robert Fisher, the lawyer who headed it, was born. The Harriman decision partly arose from a campaign publicly waged by the city's newspapers, the *Utica Observer Dispatch* and *Daily Press*, and the 1957 Apalachin raid. That raid, in which two Utica brothers, Joe and Sal Falcone were exposed, was a meeting of top mafia figures from all over the northeast in a small hamlet in the Catskill Mountains. The raid prompted the *Observer Dispatch*'s reporting and pushed the governor to action. It was a common assumption that the Elefante political machine, at the very least, enabled organized crime to operate in the city. Many outsiders considered Rufie part of it. As public pressure grew, pressure to crack the Elefante hold on Utica grew with it. The Fisher investigation story would warrant an entire book. In short, the very public exposure of corruption in Utica led to many Elefante operatives, including Uncle Denny, being criminally charged, convicted and sent to jail. Although not a legal glove was laid on Rufie, it appeared that his political control and involvement was severely damaged, when a Republican, Frank Dulan, was elected mayor in the election of 1959.

Oneida County government was also in a state of flux. There, too, reform was in the air. On the county level, reform also started to take shape within the Republican Party. That was first apparent in 1960, when the party's leadership changed. Both as a reaction to the Utica corruption scandals, the Elefante-Kirch relationship and reform minded business and political interests in the city of Rome, county government was altered from the legislative form to an executive one. In 1962, the county charter was changed and in 1963, Charles Lanigan of Rome became the first Oneida County Executive.

The Assaro Beginning

Understanding the backdrop to the Assaro period in Utica also requires reference to what can be termed the Italian factor. Utica's largest ethnic base was Italian-American, as was Rufus Elefante. Heavy doses of patronage flowed from the Elefante machine to the Italian, East Utica-based population. One cannot underscore strongly enough the top of this political pyramid, which was control of the Italian vote. Rufie gave jobs to people when they needed them most, through the Depression, WWII, and after. He took care of the Italian immigrant class and their offspring. Many families owed their economic lives to Elefante. They would not easily or quickly forget. Elefante's political machine was expanded by building a coalition of East Utica Italian-Americans and West Utica Polish-Americans. This was a powerful avenue to political control which translated into the ability to deliver both private and public sector patronage jobs. As in all history, when economic control is blended with political control, that control is nearly absolute. Rufie had one primary self-created rule; he would never allow an Italian-American mayor. Of the many mayors elected and controlled by the Elefante machine, none were Italian. The reason was obvious. An Italian mayor could build the power within the Italian community to challenge Elefante himself.

The unwillingness of Rufie to allow an Italian to lead in an elected capacity resulted in deep seeded resentment within a segment of the Italian community, particularly the young adults. Many wondered why an Italian was not good enough to be mayor. After all, were not Italians the largest ethnic group in the city? There was also a small, but educated group of Utica Italian-Americans who had always resisted Elefante's dominance. This was, in part, due to the rebellious nature of the ethnic group and the perceived embarrassment brought to Italians by the image of corruption and crime associated with their ethnic group. Such a rebel was the father of Dominick Assaro. His sons, Dominick and John, followed their father's lead.

By 1965, there were several dynamics in play that led to the challenge of the political status quo by the creation of the Assaro political group and movement. First, Frank Dulan was perceived as incompetent and unable to move Utica forward. As mentioned earlier, the city and area were losing jobs. In Utica's case, the late 1950s and early to mid 1960s saw the start of a significant flight to the suburbs. As a high school student, I experienced and assisted this flight by virtue of my 1959 summer job with the water board. We summer helpers had to actually work because it was an election year. I became part of a pipe laying crew. We both delivered water main pipe to sites and helped lay it. All of my crew work took place in the Harts Hill area of Whitesboro. Other crews worked in other suburban areas. What did this mean? Extending water meant extending housing. People were starting to move out of the city into the suburbs. In 1965, it wasn't recognized locally as the national phenomena it was and Dulan was taking a hit for the growing flight of people out of the city. The Dulan administration had also started a big downtown Urban Renewal project which was stalled. The Utica newspaper was fixated with "the downtown," and Dulan was being blamed for the development's problems and failures. Finally, and perhaps most seriously, in many quarters Dulan was thought to be in cahoots with Rufus Elefante. Stories of collusion between the two were common.

Unlike today, in those days Utica's mayoral term was two years. Even with the loss to Dulan in 1959 and subsequent losses in 1961 and 1963, the Elefante political apparatus still controlled the Democratic Party. There was the school of thought that Rufie had constructed a Potemkin village for the Democrats, who still reaped the benefits. In other words, the Republican Dulan was really a front man and played ball with, if not controlled by, Rufie. Stories floating around involved secret meetings, payoffs and land deals. One even involved Dulan receiving money from Rufie in Italy. I knew of no evidence to support that theory but that belief which was held by many combined with the economic and population decline of Utica, gave rise to the cry for what was labeled and perceived as true and complete political reform.

What Utica Needs

In 1965, Fred Nassar, Bill Lucy and Dominick Assaro wrote and published a book called *What Utica Needs*. It was a book that presented a written blueprint for economic change and revival in Utica. The book was serialized by the *Observer Dispatch*. Its overall theme was economic expansion through enlightened private and public leadership and policies. It was the first step in their plan for political takeover of the City of Utica. In modern American politics, it seems that every politician writes a book to legitimize him or herself. In 1965, the concept was novel. It elevated the image of the authors in ways that would be an advantage in the political arena.

To properly understand the Assaro political effort, the three key founders must be understood. Nassar was the strategic brains; Lucy was the writer and student of government; and Dick Assaro was the perfect candidate. Fred Nassar was briefly described earlier. It should be added that his vision was to lead the effort to control Utica, win and build new and influential state and national relationships. These relationships would then be used to advance the city and the area. Fred was a brilliant thinker. He did not have the attributes to be, nor did he desire to be a candidate. He was shy, not good looking and uncomfortable in the limelight. Bill Lucy, who came to the area as a reporter for the *Observer Dispatch*, was a highly educated, University of Chicago guy who could write extremely well and grasped 1960s government policy issues. In today's language, Bill would be described as a policy wonk. He was to Assaro what Ted Sorenson was to Jack Kennedy. Dick Assaro was warm and liked by all who met him. He had a great smile and pleasant manner with people. He always seemed interested in what others had to say. And, he was very respectful. He was a man of the neighborhood whose personality shone as his greatest attribute. He was not a policy thinker but he too was highly intelligent. His personality was important to the funeral home business he and his brother John ran since the passing of their father. Dick was the soft Assaro; John the hard more business oriented. The Assaros were also as anti-Rufie as their dad was. The family was a rare Italian Republican one. Dick had also demonstrated his vote getting stripes running for minor city offices in the late 1950s. In fact in 1959, Assaro was first publically noted as mayoral timber.

A long term relationship between Assaro and Nassar stemmed from the strong family ties of the two families. Lucy, at 25, was an add on, so to speak, who had close ties to educational, cultural and social circles who wanted to see change in Utica. The three met within these circles. It is critical to note that Nassar and Lucy were both highly personally ambitious as well. They saw themselves as people who could play a big part in the struggle for greater political good that could take them beyond Utica. This was the 1960s. It was the era of Camelot and JFK. After JFK was shot, RFK picked up the torch. Politics was the noblest of callings. "Ask not what your country can do for you..." Public service was home to the best and the brightest. Underpinning it all was the thought that society was only as good as its political leadership. Fred Nassar and Bill Lucy exemplified that 1960's thinking as did many who gravitated to the Assaro group.

1965 Primary and Elections

Pushed by concern for the city, a fierce anti Elefante stimulation and the strong reception of *What Utica Needs*, Dick Assaro announced in the spring of 1965 that he would challenge Frank Dulan in a Republican primary for Mayor of Utica. The basis of his campaign was political reform and industrial growth all built around the theme of inspiring and enlisting younger generations to help change the city. This theme was best expressed in a passage from *What Utica Needs* which said, "Our youth are not afraid to strive and lead. They have faith to pursue their dreams. Let us begin." That 1965 announcement was the formal beginning of the Assaro Movement.

Frank Dulan, who only six short years earlier was the reformer, was perceived by many as not only corrupt but as too much of an old style, backward looking politician. Dulan was your typical Irish-American politician of the 1940s and 1950s. He was a two-fisted drinker, who could belt out a tune and weave a great tale. He was rough along the edges and perceived by the Assaro people as not the brightest bulb in the lamp. Uneducated, Dulan's history included delivering ice in the early 1940s. He actually delivered to the East Utica home at which I was born. There was a sense by those who gravitated to Assaro, that Dulan was a relic of the past with no sense of modernity. The perception of his ties to Rufie Elefante has already been mentioned.

When as a graduating college student, I made the call to Dick Assaro, we were invited to meet with him at the funeral home on the following Saturday morning. Sam Vedete and I went as the Vice President and President of the Utica College Young Republican Club. In anticipating the meeting, Sam and I were struck by how easy it was for us to get a meeting with the candidate himself. We also thought it funny that we would meet in a funeral home. At the time, we did not realize that it was also the Assaro residence. We joked of having coffee and talking alongside a corpse. We also made jokes about Assaro's campaign being "dead."

When we arrived, we were met by Assaro, Nassar and Lucy. Nassar ran the meeting. We quickly learned how much we "fit" the Assaro youth theme. I vividly recall how much I was taken with these guys. Fred Nassar was so smart, pacing and chain smoking, mind rolling along like a locomotive, always chugging, thinking first, then talking. Lucy was studious, bright and erudite. Dick was warm as could be, with a smile like we were old friends. The long and the short of it is that we were flattered and impressed by them and totally committed to becoming involved. They asked about our group and our capability to deliver campaign volunteers. Also critical to them was our willingness to go public. Again, what better match than the Assaro youth movement headed by the local college Young Republicans. We agreed to help. We were assured that they did not just want us as window dressing but wanted us to become key players in the campaign. They were going to practice what they preached when they wrote and spoke of their commitment to youth in politics. Towards that end we were invited to an inner circle campaign meeting to be held at the funeral home the following Tuesday night. Sam could not go; I could, and did.

That first meeting offered a glimpse of the Assaro beginning and what it meant. I do not recall all of the participants but do recall the key ones. Of course, there was Dick, Fred and Bill. Also, there was Dick's brother John. John was also the husband of a woman who worked with my mother at Utica's premier department store, the Boston Store. So, there was a family connection. Both Johnny and his wife were very nice and friendly. He was a short, thin guy with an entertaining personality. He also had a gruff side. In addition to the funeral business, John was also active in local acting circles. There was Bill Spitzer, a local businessman, who was a very quiet, serious man who exhibited great common sense. I think his connection was with Fred more than Dick. A really nice guy named Vinnie Esposito was part of the group. I learned later that Vinnie represented and worked for a man named Marty Abelove. He was a very rich, Jewish businessman who was pledged to be the largest single financial donor to the campaign. His major business was a laundry supply company. I knew of the company when I was a student at Colgate, where the Abelove Company did the dorm sheets, pillow cases and towels. Joe Karam was in attendance. Karam was Fred's associate at Griffiss and also knew John Assaro through the Player's Theater. Joe was a big, heavy set guy who was obviously very smart and had a tendency to talk a lot. Fred had to silence him throughout the meeting. Joe would have talked the night away. I was most fascinated with Tony Fernicola. He first frightened. He was a tough looking, well dressed criminal lawyer who appeared to have a permanent, sCarey sneer on his face. This sneer, I later realized, was caused by a palsy condition. I had read about Tony's legal activities, including defending accused mob members. Fernicola was by far the best criminal lawyer in the area. More of Tony will come up later, but I quickly learned to admire, respect and cherish his friendship. He was a wonderful and brilliant man.

I was both nervous and impressed. Here I was, a 22 year old student who loved politics sitting in on the inside of a group wanting to take over the entire city! And, I could be part of it. Fooling around in college politics was one thing; being part of a real, enlightened effort to govern and control was another. The only similar feeling I had ever experienced was hitting a 25 foot jump shot to help win a big game. In other words, you got really pumped up.

The topic of that meeting was to answer the question of who Dick should ask to be his running mate as President of the Common Council. Previous meetings had boiled down the choice between a prominent local woman named Wilma Sinnot and business man named Richard Hanley. I knew of both. Wilma was the wife of a Utica banker and the head of the League of Women Voters. Hanley was a big shot at the Bendix Corporation's Utica division. Both were part of the group of reform minded people from various walks of life committed to the Assaro message and team. It is important to emphasize that all of the Assaro people were not part of the political establishment, either Democrat or Republican. They were classic, "good government" types. Party labels meant little. Dick was a registered Republican by virtue of his anti Rufie upbringing, but many of his closest supporters were Democrats. Strategically as measured and articulated by Nassar, an Italian Republican candidate would be the ultimate ideal candidate to run against a Rufie Democrat for the obvious demographic logic that a Republican who could cut into the heavily Italian Democratic vote was a sure winner. Remember, Dick would be the first Italian mayor. Step one was to beat Dulan.

The meeting was seemingly never ending. The choice was between a top notch woman popular in reform circles or in a businessman who would represent the issue of jobs and growth. Some asked the question of whether or not the city was ready for a woman candidate for a top city office. Who would bring in more voting and perhaps money was also discussed and argued. After 1:00 AM the matter was still unresolved. Tempers were flaring and Fred was losing control of the meeting. Finally, Fernicola leaped to his feet and yelled, "I've had enough, let's flip a f***in' coin." A coin was flipped and Hanley won. It was hilarious. But, there was one very telling aspect of that meeting that didn't dawn on me until years later. Dick Assaro himself did not make the ultimate choice. He left it to the group and the coin toss. He was as tired and frustrated as the rest of us.

The Campaign

There are two parts of the Assaro 1965 Republican Primary campaign that pretty much explains it all. First, the campaign was run and supported by virtually 100% volunteers. There were no party committeemen, no paid staff, no paid advisors and very few commercials. Money was tight. It was true, grass roots, anti political establishment movement. It was the first city wide campaign of both the candidate and those close to him. Second, the campaign stayed true to its theme of creating a future for young adults to grow the city. In addition to press releases and position papers largely crafted by Nassar and Lucy, the feature of the campaign was a series of neighborhood rallies held in each section of the city. Our little college group was put in charge of organizing and carrying out these rallies. We created one format that was used in each section, South, East, North, West Utica and Cornhill. Each started with music, highlighted by a live performance of what would turn out to be the infamous "Hang Down Your Head, Frank Dulan." The song, sung to the tune of the popular folk song, "Tom Dooley," was written by a very clever young guy named Tom Ciola. He sang, "Hang down your head, Frank Dulan / Hang down your head and cry / With you, Utica is goin' to die." Tom had verses tied into urban renewal failures, bad services and the exodus of the young. While he sang it, a bunch of us ran around with hand held blow horns and leaflets trying to build up the crowd. And of course, a press release was issued ahead of time for each. Opening the speeches was Professor Owen Roberts of Utica College. Owen was a wonderfully eccentric man with a learned British accent who dressed as flowery as Little Richard and who could really crank out a lively, audacious, very funny speech. I recall him at a huge rally on the corner of Bleecker and Albany Streets, in the heart of East Utica, calling Rufie Elefante, the "Il Duce, Pearl Mesta of Catherine Street!" It made no sense, but brought the house down. Roberts was followed by one of us college students saying how much young people like us believed in Utica and Dick Assaro. We alternated by neighborhood. Sam Vedete in East Utica because he was Italian, me in Polish West Utica, Bob North in North Utica. Dick came on last and presented his plan for Utica's rebirth and asked for votes. We finished each with chants to vote for Dick. One rally took on a particular significance.

Prior to the East Utica rally, Mayor Dulan issued a press statement implying that Assaro had Mafia backing. Dick used the rally to condemn Dulan's remarks by reaching his arms out to all of us young people saying, "Look at these young college graduates or those soon to graduate. Are they Mafia?" He went on to further condemn Dulan's remarks as anti Italian and insulting to all the young Italian Americans who were giving their time and effort for the future of Utica. Dick's appearance, his remarks and the rally received local front page press coverage. Our little college group could not have been prouder or more excited. We were to be disappointed.

Dick lost the primary 5,500 to 3,150. As Fred looked at the results, he concluded that it was an excellent run considering little money, no formal party support and our lack of experience. He and the other insiders felt that there was nothing to lose and everything to gain by running as an independent in the November election. Nassar brilliantly saw that Dick, as an independent, could throw a real dent into the traditional Democratic East Utica. If he could garner a decent splint among more independent Republicans and attract new non affiliated voters, victory was possible. But, most did realize that victory was a tremendous long shot. The real goal was to make sure Rufie would lose. Dick was young, Dulan was old and Rufie might be knocked out with another loss. Dick, if he showed strength as a third party candidate, could solidify a future role in the city's leadership, if not another run.

Dick ran under what was registered, The Progress Party. He also had the Liberal line. Dulan won the election by about 3,000 votes and Dick came close to beating the Democratic candidate by getting only 100 votes less than that candidate. It was clear that Dick's presence on the ballot did cost Rufie's candidate the election by the East Utica vote split we anticipated.

One of the funniest anecdotes of the campaign was the Liberal Party endorsement. To this day, I don't know where it came from and how it was delivered to Dick. I recall being in headquarters one day as two trench coated, Leon Trotsky looking types walked in. They were Liberal Party operatives from New York City here to "advise" the campaign. They were in and out several times that summer. They were never without trench coats. They were also very funny and very nice guys. We Young Republicans would scratch our heads over our alignment with the "downstate communists!" We went from mafia to commies in one fell swoop!

It was during this summer that I also got to better know and catch a young man's worship fever of Tony Fernicola. Since HQ was downtown, as was Tony's office, he stopped in virtually every day and most evenings. I volunteered there on a pretty full time basis. Fernicola would wax eloquently about everything from crime stories related to his clients, to the Congressional Mafia hearings of a few years before and philosophy from St. Augustine to Kant to Marx. He was simply one of the most interesting people I've ever met. I learned more from him that summer than I learned in years of college. For a young man, it was like sitting at the feet, listening to the master. As he walked into headquarters, he would growl, "The ice man cometh; the ice man goeth." His literary take off quickly became repeated by those of us who fancied our intellectual prowess.

I also learned some practical, eye opening politics. I and others were asked to sign affidavits that we gave Assaro certain sums of money which we did not really donate. These fake statements were designed to cover the financial contributions of Marty Abelove who did not want to be publically identified with Assaro. He did not want to hurt his businesses or those friends and family members who supported Rufie. His brother, Milt, for example, was a big, long time Rufie confidant and real estate partner. While working at a Bleecker Street voting place in the heart of East Utica the day of the primary, I saw the mayor's forces buying votes for $5 right out in the open. I was too frightened to say a word. And, tomatoes thrown at us at Assaro rallies made a point. We were challenging some tough customers who were protecting their city jobs. These tastes of street politics were highly educational in ways not taught in the classroom.

It was a period never forgotten. It was a summer that hatched the Assaro movement and gave this author a political taste of power that whetted the appetite to eat and drink more of it. I envisioned being a Fred or Bill, a Tony or even a thin version of Joe Karam. It was a vision of being a behind the scenes master planner in the arena of political power. I took this appetite with me as I left for graduate school to study theoretical politics and mechanics of government administration.

The 1967 Election

Before getting into the campaign details, it is necessary to expand on my personal situation mentioned earlier. When I transferred into UC, I carried a full load in school, worked at various jobs, played some sports and got involved in student government. By the time I graduated in 1965, I had three kids, the last being born in April of that year. So, I was already married, with a family as I got involved with the Assaro group. All took to each other very quickly in a certain kind of bonding. My wife and kids got to know both Dick and many others of the group. Largely through the efforts of a wonderful political science professor, Dr. Bob Anderson, I received a fellowship offer from a school called the Graduate School of Public Affairs at Albany. At the time, it was part of a combined Union College and State University program of an accelerated Masters program in political science or public affairs. It was in later years absorbed totally by the State of New York and is now part of the University at Albany.

I studied and commuted home nearly every weekend. There was steady contact with the Assaro people. Knowing that Dick was going to run again, I wanted to begin my working career in Utica. But, I had four mouths to feed and had to take the first decent job offer I got as I neared completion of my studies. I was also intent on a government career. As I received an offer from a downstate city, Bill Lucy arranged for a meeting with Oneida County Planning Department officials who had an opening. Bill knew, liked and respected these guys. Chuck Lanigan, the new Oneida County Executive, had recruited a top notch planning director named Dave Brandon. Municipal Planning in those days was the cat's meow of modern, forward looking, government and Lanigan wanted to build a great department. Brandon was very smart, accomplished, well known in municipal planning circles and a really nice guy. He, in turn, was recruiting a talented staff, virtually all from outside of the area. I was interviewed by Brandon and his second in command, Jim Barwick, another bright guy. I thought the interview went well but I didn't think I would get an offer. I really thought some Republican would find out and veto any chance I had with the Republican Lanigan administration because of my Assaro affiliation. I was wrong and got an offer which I accepted. Upon finishing my studies in the fall of 1966, I would become a Planning Specialist involved in zoning administration and ordinance creation in subunits within the county. I also specialized in helping units identify state and federal grant programs. I often wondered why I was never called to task for my Assaro affiliation. Maybe I was too small a fish. Perhaps more important was that there was no love lost between Lanigan and Dulan.

So, that is the backdrop to what was unfolding in Utica all built around the decision by Assaro to run for mayor again in 1967. What was behind this decision makes for fascinating politics that extended way beyond Utica and altered people's lives forever. More than anything, I wanted to be a part of that and took the County Planning job for that reason. I wanted to help finish what was started two years before; the political takeover of Utica.

The Assaro Decision

Then and now, it seems obvious that only one path was clear to take. That path was for Assaro to change political parties and to run as a Democrat. At the time Utica Democrats outnumbered Republicans by about 8,000.In his independent run, Dick demonstrated that he could attract significant Democrat votes where they counted most, East Utica. His experiences as a Republican since the late 1950s also told a story that the Republican Party hierarchy and political structure were not ready to embrace an East Utica Italian. It is also critical to remember that the only reason Assaro was a Republican was that he and his family were anti Rufie Elefante. Ideologically, Dick and his key supporters, including Nassar, Lucy, Fernicola and others were classic liberal Democrats. In my initial exposure to the group, I was constantly reminded that I was alone as a bona fide Goldwater, conservative Republican.

The thinking of the Assaro brain trust was that if Dick could win the Democrat nomination, he could retain the reform Republican support he had and easily win the mayoral prize. Another element, which would become the most important element in the entire Assaro story, was the Kennedy factor. All elements combined in the perception that a win and the final triumph over the Elefante influence were not only possible, but likely. The Democratic Party label was essential.

The Kennedy Connection

In 1964, Bobby Kennedy was elected United States Senator from New York, defeating Ken Keating. Back in the days when Bobby was U.S. Attorney General in his brother's cabinet, he was a committed anti-mob prosecutor. There was a long standing belief that Utica was a mob haven and that Rufus Elefante was mob connected. Although that was never proven in any legal way, Kennedy himself believed it and had disdain for the Utica Democratic Party controlled by Rufie. As the Assaro shift was becoming a reality, Nassar, the brilliant strategist, sensed a potential alliance and had written a couple of letters to the Senator and his key staffers. They were met with interest. The whole Kennedy mystique of bright, young, dedicated people remaking the nation and the world fit the Assaro vision of bright, young people remaking Utica. Finally, there was a deep civil rights strain in both Nassar and Lucy and they viewed RFK through that prism as well. The Kennedy connection would also fit Nassar's central political goal of establishing major league national relationships for Utica. You couldn't get more major league than the Kennedys. Meetings were quickly arranged through Kennedy reps in Syracuse and New York City and the seeds of a political alliance were sown. By 1966, the framework for a Kennedy/Assaro allegiance was established which would become a key part of the Assaro political movement and its future. Not only could we get the benefit of the Kennedy name; we could also get some huge help in running campaigns. The Kennedys had a sophisticated machine which could be a huge help to the Assaro group. The first step was the political party switch. We became Kennedy Democrats.

The 1967 Campaign

Soon after his formal registration change, Dick announced his candidacy for mayor. The Elefante wing of the party nominated Sebastian "Sal" Convertino. Thus the stage was set for a showdown in the party primary to be held in September. After a political blood bath that literally split Italian families between the young and the old, Assaro squeaked out a victory. The difference was a sparse 102 votes. That demonstrated that there was still a lot of life in the Elefante machine. And, Convertino was a young, attractive Italian-American candidate in his own right. In backing Convertino, Rufie finally realized he could no longer avoid the historical evolution to an Italian-American mayor. The city's largest population group had reached its time to demand an elected leader and not to be content with an unelected boss. Since Convertino was on the November ballot on the Liberal line, the general election figured to be equally close. It turned out to be what may have been the most dramatic, interesting election in the history of Utica! It had all the elements of a great drama: mob issues, Kennedy glamour, young vs. old, reform vs. establishment. And, it was bitter.

The Assaro campaign stole a page out of the Kennedy play book and ran on a "we can do better" platform. It was a platform based on a vision for the future, tying right back into Assaro's 1965 theme. Dulan ran his usual clumsy campaign, again relying on his "mobster" innuendos. That theme looked really stupid when Bobby Kennedy not only endorsed Dick, but came to Utica in October to campaign for him. The Kennedy rally was amazing in its fervor. Kennedy brought the house down when he pledged not to cut his long hair until Dick Assaro was elected Mayor of Utica! RFK was electrifying, to say the least.

As I was writing this book, I met with several people still around from the Assaro days. One was Fred Nassar's brother, Gene. He is highly intelligent, literary expert and one of the best pure teachers in the history of Utica College. As we were talking about the Kennedy visit, Gene shook his head and remarked that he couldn't take his eyes off those of Bobby Kennedy when he came to Utica in 1967. Gene saw such intensity in Kennedy's eyes that he wondered if he was, "on something." I found that very interesting and related an "eyes" story of my own to Gene. I once watched Jack Nicklaus play in the US Senior Open at the Ridgewood Country Club in New Jersey in the mid 1990s. One of my friends was a member and secured the tickets. A man who was to be my boss one day was with us. He knew Jack. So, we followed Nicklaus all day. I could not take my eyes off his. I never saw such intensity. Nicklaus was in a zone all to himself. He had no idea what was going on around him. It was the most amazing ability to focus and you could see it in his eyes. He was in a rare and special zone of intensity. He wasn't on anything but the competition. I told Gene, that I bet what he saw in RFK's eyes was the same thing. It separates the great from the very good. Kennedy's appearance, only one of two he made for a mayoral race in the nation, gave Dick a huge boost and really energized his base. We felt that both our effort and Utica were in the big leagues.

Interestingly, Sal Convertino did not, until the end of the campaign, wage an active campaign from his Liberal line. No one understood the thinking behind this lack of effort but Convertino was quiet until Rufie himself came out publically against Dick. By then, any impact Convertino could have had was gone. In my research for this book, I interviewed Convertino and asked him why he did not wage a vigorous third line campaign from the outset. He indicated that no matter what "the old man" felt, he did not have it in him to be just a spoiler. Of course, the "old man" reference was of Elefante and he was bent on keeping victory from Assaro. Ethnic ties did not matter. My sense is that they did matter to Sal.

The icing on the campaign cake was the endorsement of the Utica newspapers. They finally deserted their former champion, Frank Dulan. They endorsed Dick Assaro. The *Observer Dispatch* endorsement was important for several reasons. The primary one was its refutation of the Mafia claims Dulan continued to make against Dick. The *Observer Dispatch*, which exposed the city crime and corruption within Utica in the first place, would certainly not endorse the candidate of the mob. The Dulan claim was thus rendered silly.

On the first Tuesday in November, 1967, Dick Assaro was elected mayor of the City of Utica. The Assaro movement, started by the few, won the control of an entire city. The first step in the plan for reform and growth for Utica was accomplished. And, perhaps most important of all, Utica had its first Italian-American mayor! History was made.

The 1968-1969 Term

The Assaro group entered City Hall in January, 1968 with two primary goals in mind: to build a political power base that would stretch beyond Utica and to use this expanded political power to grow the city economically. This growth in turn would have a positive impact on the city's social structure. As I look back on the time, it was surprising and telling that basic city services were rarely discussed.

There were a couple of vital components deemed necessary to attain our goals. The first was to build a highly competent staff; the second to strengthen and expand the Kennedy relationship. To understand these goals, one has to understand the strengths and thinking of Fred Nassar. In his excellent book, *Close to Power*, Bill Lucy said of Nassar, "I also learned from Nassar that politics and policy could form a rich brew." Lucy went on to describe Fred's ability to examine and dissect approaches to problem solving and, more important, his strategic thinking to assure implementation. As Lucy put it, "a plan destined for the shelf was unthinkable." What this translated to was to create the talent and relationships based on a politics of action, designed to both advance the city and the Assaro team.

During the transition period between the election and taking the oath of office, Assaro, Nassar and Lucy started to build their team. Both Nassar and Lucy were to take jobs in City Hall, Fred as Corporation Counsel and Bill in the Urban Renewal Department as a communications head. Locally, Lou Critelli was talked into taking a sabbatical from GE to become City Engineer. Joe Karam left his job at Griffiss to become Assistant to the Mayor. I was dying to work for the administration and it was arranged for me and a person named Jim Kennedy to come over from County Planning and start the city's first Planning Department. I was deemed too young and inexperienced to be director and became Jim's assistant.

Several things are important to note about these "local" appointments. All hired had advanced levels of education and all had participated in the political aspect of the Assaro rise. And, perhaps most important, all by then were friends, some longer and deeper than others, but nevertheless friends. This translated into a deep commitment of loyalty to Dick and to the group as a whole. It was understood and planned that this group would straddle professional jobs with politics. These were to be the core of the administration; those closest to the mayor. This model of educated professionals operating in the government and also running the politics of the Administration was taken right out of the Kennedy play book.

For other positions, people with outstanding professional credentials were brought in from the outside, meaning from outside of the city and outside of the then immediate Assaro political family. These included the Public Safety Commissioner, Hillard Trubitt, a professional from Indiana recommended by the Kennedys, Charley Cole, a traffic and parking wizard from New Haven, an Urban Development Director from Canada, Bill Haigis, and others.

Locals recruited who were not part of the Assaro political group included Jim Senor, who left his position as head of the Jewish Community Center to become Personnel Director, Jim Kiernan and Sue Baum. Joe Julian was recruited from Syracuse. Joe also had some ties to the pro Kennedy forces there and was experienced in Syracuse city affairs and at Syracuse University. As I recall a title was created for him that had little to do with his overall general advisory role.

All of those hired were bright, highly professional and representatives of a new breed of educated, young, dedicated local level public servants. They were not all hired at the very start of the new administration but came at later stages. Assaro and his key advisors were making the statement that there was a new level of professionalism dawning in Utica city government. Only two of this group were to also be involved in political decision making and operations.

One appointment that made little sense on paper but came to be understood quickly in the term was that of the appointment of Jim Benedetto as Public Works Commissioner. Jim was a capable guy but had no credentials or experience to handle that particular job. He was a straight on political appointment. The importance of that job in the Assaro administration would later become clear. It involved a political motive we were supposed to be above.

Overall though, it is unarguable that the team assembled was the most qualified group of people to ever work in Utica City Hall. Today, when the Assaro period is mentioned, the first comment is usually that "he had the best staff ever."

The immediate political ingredient of the brew boiled down to Bobby Kennedy and his organization. 1968 was a Presidential election year. It was understood and planned for several years that RFK was going to run for President. Lyndon Johnson's announcement that he would not seek reelection pushed Bobby into the race in 1968.

The Assaro group was expected to help in several ways. It was time to pay back. Coordinating the interaction was Jerry Bruno, who was JFK's lead advance man and an RFK organizer. The other direct contact was Steve Smith, a Kennedy brother-in-law, based in New York City. Virtually all upstate cities were then controlled by either Republican mayors or old-guard, tainted Democrats. Recognizing both the talent and reformist zeal of the Assaro group, the Kennedys looked to us to help lead an upstate Kennedy controlled Democratic political organization that would deliver the New York nomination and primary votes to RFK.

The President Robert Kennedy scenario offered a quick opportunity for the Nassar national influence plan to be realized. Imagine the benefits that could come to Utica from a close Kennedy alliance. If Kennedy were to be elected President in 1968 or at worst, four years later, the sky would be the limit for Utica. Receiving major infrastructure and institutional improvements like a major north-south highway, an engineering degree school tied to RADC, significant housing related grants, and the like would all be achievable. In other words, political power would bring the goals described in *What Utica Needs*, to reality. Utica would be on the national map. So would Assaro and his team. There was already talk of a judgeship or state party chairmanship for Nassar. And some of us had dreams and thoughts of going to DC to be part of the Kennedy national reawakening. Such was the dream.

Decision Making

The decision making process at the very outset of the new administration was basically the same as that of the campaign. It was to gather respected and trusted people in a room and discuss the issue to its fullest, soliciting opinions from all. Who was in the room was sometimes dependent on the issue itself but nearly always included Nassar, Lucy, Karam and, of course, the mayor. Often, the mayor's brother John was included. I was sharing my time between the planning and mayor's office and was also included most of the time. Lou Critelli's opinion quickly grew in value, as did his presence in the mayor's office. Normally, Fred ran the meetings, pacing, chain smoking, questioning participants, and mediating disputes. One thing was perfectly clear to all. Anybody could say anything in the room but once a decision was made, all were to support it and make it happen. Loyalty to the process and the group was paramount. It was not to be violated. This covered political and administrative matters. Although the discussion sessions were mostly serious, they were also a lot of fun. I remind the reader that we were all friends outside of the room and building. And no one was shy about going after another, often in a cutting, sarcastic way.

Joe Karam generated a lot of the laughs and frustrations. As pointed out earlier, Joe was ultra bright and completely undisciplined. He was a big guy and always eating. He would usually rush into a meeting with something in his mouth while jumping into the conversation that had started before his arrival. He quickly was labeled the "Answer Man." He offered an answer before he knew the question! This drove Fred and Dick nuts while the rest of us would laugh and start verbally assaulting Joe. Dick Assaro would coin a phrase he would use frequently over the next few years: "Joey, what are you doing to me?"

One cannot truly understand Karam without understanding that his greatest love was that of food. Joe Karam eating stories could fill an entire book, pun intended. I'll tell but one. Joe ate a lot and did not have the best of table manners. In other words, he ate fast and furiously. I recall a dinner stop at a fancy restaurant in Albany after a meeting with state officials. The place was packed with political movers and shakers. Joe ordered a full lobster and decimated it in record time. Shells and lobster bits flew as he tore into it. At finish time, the entire dining room full of people spontaneously stood and applauded. Joe bowed and waved; Dick was mortified.

An important fact that was not understood by those outside of City Hall, was that the mayor had the final say in all decisions. That may sound trite and obvious, but the perception of many was that Dick was just a figurehead run by Fred Nassar. That was not the case. Fred respected the mayor and the mayor's position. Fred was no boss. And, Dick had an inner strength that could be deceiving. The force of Nassar's thinking and arguments often carried the day, but Dick had to put the final stamp of approval on all major decisions. I quickly came to understand that Dick Assaro was no pushover.

To repeat an earlier point, strategies and decisions were always based on what could be done efficiently and quickly. A long term master planning type approach would be laughed out of the room. That developed as a barrier between the core group and many of the out of town bureaucrats brought in. I remember Dick frequently asking one of us after including one of our imports into a discussion, "What the hell was he saying? I couldn't understand a word."

It is also important to understand that decisions affecting the city were always discussed with outside interests, most usually the business community before the mayor made them. Dick would invariably call in a Charley George who headed GE and or Jack Kennelly who represented the Chamber of Commerce to solicit opinions and support. Utica's industrial base was impressive and its importance was not overlooked or neglected. Those meetings usually included the mayor, one aid and the business guys. GE employed about 8,000 people, many of whom lived in Utica. George was a very influential and a smart guy to boot. The way Assaro treated him was indicative of a mayor who would not make a decision on any matter of city wide importance without reaching out to the business community. Dick understood where the jobs and money were.

Common Council votes were always counted and lobbied. Garnering Council support for legislation was extremely difficult. Democrats were in the majority but they were by and large old guard Rufie Democrats. Frank Andrello, the Majority Leader, Tony Garramone, Fred Trino, Red Weresynski and Jim Byrne were not warm to us. There were some pluses. Andrello loved to be courted, loved to deal and always wanted something. You could do business with him. Garramone was smart and although he had a volatile temper, could be talked to. The rest were followers with anti Assaro agendas. The Republicans were interesting. Their leader, Rex Gilliland, was a reform Republican who had an affinity for Assaro when Dick was a Republican. Rex was smart and articulate. Gordon Hathaway, representing North Utica, was also reasonable and not a party line guy. Bob Lynch was, and he had mayoral ambition. The point is that voting coalitions could be built but the building took hard work and horse-trading. We never went to the Council unless it was absolutely required and we worked very hard to deliver votes when we had to. Implementation was everything.

Under most circumstances, politics in Utica City Hall trumped policy because of the two year mayoral term. No sooner when you were in office did you have to start thinking about and planning for the next election. The old adage that the first thought a candidate has once he wins is of reelection was magnified in Utica because of the short term. The Kennedy connection and the 1968 national election elevated political concerns to a level way above what they would have been had we not been involved with them. Of course, it is possible Dick Assaro would have not been elected without the Kennedy support. As they say, in for a dime, in for a dollar.

A Great Time

What could be better than a bunch of young guys who had a hell of a good time together running a city? Our inner group, minus Lucy, was a hard drinking, gambling, golf loving bunch. Dick Assaro himself would bet on anything that moved. He loved all forms of gambling. We had, as they say today, swagger. Card games were held inside and outside of City Hall. When Dick got bored or had some free time, he'd take some of us to the bomb shelter to play knock rummy. The day before holidays, there were often a couple of card games going on in the mayor's office. I recall one Good Friday when I played poker hands in two rooms. Friends like Patty Basile and Bernie Turi would drop in and perform a Don Rickles style comedy routine worthy of Vegas. Many nights, we had many gin or pinochle games at my house. Why my house? My wife loved the guys and they loved her. She didn't mind the crowd or the mess. Friday nights always featured dinner at Nash's restaurant on Bleecker Street. I always brought my wife and Joe Karam even started dating her sister. A Friday night at Nash's usually included the best veal dishes ever, anywhere, a lot of wine and a spoon playing concert by Frankie Nash after the place closed. Rocco Benedetto carried on about old Utica gambling and crime stories. Karam told his specialized jokes as only he could.

Rock Benedetto, brother of Jim, was in my opinion one of Utica's all time great "characters." As a young man, he was one of the first Italian Americans to receive a scholarship to attend Hamilton College. He chucked his studies to help run crap games in Utica and places like Saratoga Springs. Two of the stories he liked to tell deserve mention here. The first was of him and his "business partner" in the late 1940s, a guy named Fred Morelli. He and Benedetto ran a gambling business at a club in Utica. They were young rebels in the sense that their business was not sanctioned by, nor did it pay tribute to the mob. They not only defied the ruling order in that way, but loved to strut about, advertising their defiance. According to Rock, Morelli paid with his life when he was shot outside of his club. Rock claimed that his life was spared by a vote taken after an old "mustache Pete," a term for a mob elder, spoke up for him. Benedetto claimed that he was severely beaten instead. I don't know how much of this was true but it was sure fascinating to hear about it at two in the morning, sipping espresso at Frankie Nash's. The backdrop to a story like this as it related to politics and the whole Assaro group is also interesting. To those on the inside, it was kind of comical that Frank Dulan cried Mafia all the time when he was challenged by Dick. A guy like Benedetto was attracted to Dick for the opposite reason. They represented the small group, who for one reason or another, rebelled against the mob and their protector as they saw him, Rufie Elefante. They viewed Rufie as the political boss that controlled the city, gave organized crime a license to exist and operate. Dick's challenge to Rufie is what appealed to these types of Italian American rebels.

Another of Rock's great stories is what I call the peppers and eggs ego trap. After he left Hamilton College to run crap games at night, Rock had a day job clerking for a local lawyer. The office he worked at was located in the old First Bank Building, as Uticans referred to the First National Bank office building in downtown Utica. Rocco related how he secured a safety deposit box at a bank across the street in which he'd put his crap game profits every morning on his way to work. He was afraid to leave the money at home because he didn't want his mother to find out that he was up to no good. Every day, his mother would make him a fried peppers and egg sandwich to take for lunch, figuring it would help her son save lunch money. Rock, dressed in a sharp suit, French cuffed white shirt and tie would walk to the bank, toss the peppers and egg sandwich and head to the safety deposit box with the cash. He related how great it felt when the bank guard greeted him by saying, "Good morning Mr. Benedetto," as he opened the door and escorted him to the private safety box area.

There came a time when for some reason, the crap game was shut down for a long period. So, Rock's trips to the bank were to take money out, not to deposit it. Quickly, the safety deposit box was emptied. But, as Rock put it, he was addicted to the feeling of importance he had walking into that bank and being greeted by the guard. So, as he continued his routine sans cash, he deposited the peppers and eggs wrappings into the box! He did this until he could no longer pay for the box. Rock wasn't the only one of us who overdid in certain ways.

When the Saratoga thoroughbred racing meet opened in August, we'd get the Albany mayor's box once in awhile and hit the track. One trip there represents a classic Dick Assaro gambling story. Dick, Joe, Buddy Gigliotti, Rock and I went to the track one day. Sitting next to our box were two elderly, very refined women, obviously upper crust. As we had a few drinks and bet a few races, we started kidding around with them. Buddy started to assist them by running their bets to the window for them. We introduced ourselves and the mayor. They were women from one of the famous racing families. They told us that they had horses on the card and that their husbands were in the stables.

As time wore on and we all drank and had some laughs, they informed us that their horse's race was coming up and that they were confident it would win. One of us was bold enough to ask what they liked with it. As I recall, they gave us two other horses. The race was late on the card and by the time they told us we had not cashed a winner and were a little low on money; at least I was. We bet their horse straight on top with the other two horses and cashed nice paying exactas. We all won hundreds of dollars. After a great dinner, we were ready to go home winners. At dinner we saw and met The Carpenters, super stars in those days. Karen was eating!

The day was not enough for the mayor. He insisted on going to the harness track, which was running an evening card. He was the boss. We went. Buddy and I were drunk and tired and decided to sleep in the car while the others went in. Dick wound up losing all he had won at the flats and drove home totally pissed off. We lambasted him for never being happy with pocketing at least some winnings. We could speak to our leader that way because we were all so personally close and he knew at heart we were thinking of his best interests. But, the bottom line was that he was a fun guy who did not mind some back and forth ribbing.

Could it get any better? We worked and played hard. We were personally very close. We were political big shots, fun loving, wining and dining guys having one hell of a good time while saving the world. We were leading a city with flavor and character, immersed in a culture of hard work while having a lot of laughs and loving every minute of it. None of us realized how fleeting the good times would be. We thought they would last forever.

Political Change

It wasn't very long into the term after the 1967 election when I started to notice a lot of the old Rufie gang shuffling into and out of City Hall and the mayor's office. A few important and telling things became clear. The Kennedy connection was pushing us into the traditional political arena. We were going to seek the formal control of both the city and county Democratic committees because we would need those votes for the Kennedy endorsement. Party committees produce endorsements by nominating delegates to the national convention. Committeeman votes can be bought with patronage. Although positions can be challenged through primaries, it is much easier if the party apparatus is controlled and primaries avoided. The votes of the New York State delegation to the national convention were to be critical to winning the nomination. Being now in charge of the largest city in Oneida County, it was almost natural to rise to assume county wide control.

The key role of putting it all together fell to Fred Nassar. Fred became the centerpiece of this effort. As I look back on it, there was not really another who could do it. Dick was mayor. Bill was not political. John Assaro had no base or the right image. We would have had to create and rely on an outsider as a front man. Not only was there no such animal, but that wasn't our style or that of the Kennedys. Fred Nassar then became both a candidate for Chairman of the Oneida County Democratic Party, and the upstate coordinator of Bobby Kennedy's presidential campaign. This was a major step and accomplishment for us, Fred and Utica. We were in close position with one of the most powerful political groups in the history of America and we had little doubt that the White House would be won. Utica would be on the national map in many ways and forms. Major accomplishments could be realized. Nassar who was thought of locally as the power behind the Assaro throne was now out front. This was to have major ramifications for him and all connected to the Assaro team.

Locally, it quickly proved to be trouble. Both inside and outside of City Hall political realities became disheartening to the true believers. People who we fought against for years were now being given jobs for committee votes. Many of these jobs were at the

DPW which did explain why Jim Benedetto was named commissioner. We were no longer the politically pure reformers. We had lost our innocence.

Spring of 1968

In a bitter battle for control of the Democratic county chairmanship, Fred Nassar lost. He was beaten by a coalition of Rufie supporters and a group of suburban Democrats who did not want the party run by Uticans. Both groups were aligned with LBJ and ultimately Hubert Humphrey. In this battle for control, we and Fred made some lasting enemies. Many claimed that all this was unnecessary if Fred had conceded the chairmanship to another, in this case a businessman named Dominick Jiampiatro, thus building a compromise coalition. But, we could not nor would not desert the Kennedys.

Tragedy

All came crashing down on June 5, 1968. Bobby Kennedy was assassinated at a hotel in California. I recall going to bed that night knowing that RFK had won the California primary, which meant that he was most likely going to win the national nomination. Because of the time difference, I went to bed right after he was declared the winner on TV. That morning, I was halfway down the stairs to have breakfast and go to work when I encountered my sobbing wife who broke the news to me. I was stunned beyond belief. Bobby Kennedy was dead!

After hesitating briefly to watch the TV, I showered and rushed to City Hall. All I recall is that everything seemed to stop while we sat like zombies in front of a big TV that was brought into the mayor's conference room. Press relations were run out of there and calls flowed in from all over. Some of our people, for example Joe

Karam, had even been loaned to the RFK campaign and were literally out in the field. Shock, disappointment, sadness, no words are adequate to describe how we were feeling. People were running around City Hall and in the streets crying their eyes out. Bobby Kennedy and Utica did have a special friendship.

The funeral train to Virginia included a strong Utica delegation headed by Dick and Fred. I cannot comprehend nor know what this meant to the nation. As stated previously, I have little doubt that Bobby Kennedy would have been elected President. What is absolutely clear is that with his death, Utica suffered one of the most significant losses in the city's history. History is a funny thing. When the stars align and things fall into place amazing accomplishments can be achieved. One shot by an unknown, communist sympathizing whack job altered history in a way that robbed Utica of a unique opportunity to grow and prosper. And, it also altered the lives of many in the Assaro group.

The Political Aftermath

After the assassination, the presidential nomination process boiled down to a contest between Vice President Hubert Humphrey and Sen. Eugene McCarthy. Interestingly, both were from Minnesota. We quickly became part of the HHH camp. One of Humphrey's top political guys, Jack English obviously recognized New York's importance and was familiar with our group. He courted and recruited Assaro directly.

Dick became a Humphrey delegate to the 1968 Democratic National Convention in Chicago to be later infamous for its riots, Mayor Daley and the whole backdrop of Vietnam. But there is one funny story about Dick at the convention. Ever the politician, he started following Sander Vanocer, the head NBC television floor reporter. He wanted TV time. Whenever Vanocer came on camera, Dick was right there behind him. I could imagine viewers asking who that little guy always in the camera shot was. As a group of us watched that first night, we fell on the floor laughing and crying tears. Dick was a TV hound and a Vanocer stalker! Finally, one night you could see Vanocer turn around and say something to Dick. Dick quickly disappeared. When he called in the next day, we asked him what Vanocer said. Dick was told that NBC would get him thrown off the floor of the convention if he didn't stay away! I was a delegate to the 2008 Republican National Convention and while there my thoughts turned to Dick. I found myself always trying to get in a position where a TV camera was likely to pick me up. There is something about the history and drama of it all that brings out the ham in most. It was decades later but I finally fully understood Dick's funny conduct 40 years earlier.

Opportunity Strikes Twice

In the fall campaign, HHH trailed Nixon in the polls at first by a wide margin. As time wore on, the gap lessened but Nixon kept a lead. A Humphrey campaign rally was scheduled in Utica in early October. We were put in charge of organizing it with the HHH staff. We had struck a close relationship with them by then. They recognized that we did things well and New York state votes were up for grabs. The Humphrey people thought that if they could dent the upstate vote, they could carry the state. Today, you might ask, why come to Utica? Nelson Rockefeller was governor and virtually all upstate cities had Republican mayors. So, Utica made sense. The campaign came up with a brilliant gimmick to attract people for a HHH rally, which was to be held at the Utica Auditorium. Humphrey decided to make a stop in upstate New York and selected Utica. That was an honor in itself.

The Auditorium was a pretty small venue for that event. So, we created a special rule to get in. You had to have a little white, VIP lapel pin. We circulated invitations to the rally all over upstate with pins while indicating in the invitation to attend that one would indeed be "special" due to the pin. In other words, not just anyone could get in see and hear HHH. We sent pins to county Democratic Party chairs all over the state, to elected Democrats going as low as alderman. As word got out about the pins, everyone wanted one and we were flooded with calls. Anyone who asked got one. Our gimmick was based on Jerry Bruno's method of using a small venue and then over packing it thus creating an overflow image.

The sight when Humphrey arrived was amazing! The auditorium, which held about six thousand, was packed to the rafters and there were over a thousand standing outside clamoring to get in. Bus loads of people had come in from all over Upstate. I was sitting in the front row when Humphrey walked in. The crowd was as raucous as I've ever seen, cheering, stomping, making noise. It had been warmed up by the actress Shelly Winters followed by Tommy James and the Shondels, a popular rock band. Every time I hear the song Crystal Blue Persuasion, I think of that night.

With a bright gleam in his eye, HHH gave a rousing speech and brought the already whipped up house down. As he finished, he started shaking hands with those sitting on the stage. Dick motioned a few of us over to meet him. He introduced me as the guy in charge of securing grants for the city. Hubert shook my hand as he looked at me and said, "Whatever Utica wants, Utica gets."

A couple days later we called his Vice Presidential office to get help on a big housing related grant we were considering submitting to the feds. I'll never forget it. I was told, "You have the grant. Just submit the paper work and it's yours." In other words, what we wanted it for wasn't important, nor was the federal review; Utica was going to get whatever it wanted. Word had already found its way to the Vice President's staff. I guess today it would be called an earmark.

What drew Humphrey to Utica was only completely understood when Teddy White's book, *The Making of a President, 1968*, came out. In it, White quotes Humphrey as saying that he was discouraged and depressed about his campaign until the Utica rally gave him new life. His spirits rose as did his campaign fortunes. Sadly, for us and Utica it wasn't enough and he lost by a whisker to Nixon. Humphrey never forgot Utica or Dick Assaro.

For the second time in less than a year, Utica lost an opportunity for a powerful political connection that may have helped create growth and prosperity. With a Republican President and Republican governor, the city was not going to get a dime of any consequence. Major infrastructure strides relating to education, roadways, military spending, housing, etc., were not going to take place in the city. The political connections had disappeared first through tragedy, second via the national ballot box. In my opinion, far worse was to happen.

A Political Assassination

In February, 1969, Fred Nassar was indicted. This politically motivated character assassination of one of the most altruistic Uticans to ever get involved in the city's political arena was to have a profound impact on us both administratively and personally. The personal impacts were to be crushing and heart breaking.

The indictment hit most of us as a bolt of lightning. Nassar was accused of trying to solicit a political campaign contribution in trade for the contract to collect garbage in the city. Eight months later, it took a jury about an hour to clear him of all charges. To this day, reading accounts of the trial, clearly result in the inescapable conclusion that Fred's indictment was a political lynching designed to bring down the Assaro administration. Much of the testimony against Fred bordered on the laughable. It was and is clear, at least too many then, and to this writer now, that the combination of the 1968 Presidential election year and a Republican District Attorney, led to the charges. The damages wrought by this witch hunt were to be devastating to Fred and to the entire Assaro dream.

Anyone who knew Fred Nassar knew he was the man Tom Caramadre had once described in a Utica newspaper column, "Money and success are unimportant, honor is all that matters." Fred lived his life that way. He had held a high level position with the federal government at Griffiss, was a Harvard graduate but lived an unassuming life in East Utica, his birthplace. In years of overseeing procurement at a huge air base, not one blemish appeared on his record. Those who listened to him speak were entranced by his inspirational words of public service and commitment to community. To think for a second that he would throw away all he stood for money did not know Fred Nassar.

The effects of this sad, disgraceful period in Utica's history were crippling to Fred. As I knew and watched him during and after the ordeal, I have always believed that the trial was the primary reason for his untimely death in 1974 at the age of 52. But the immediate effect then was what was taking place in City Hall.

From his indictment to his acquittal, Nassar was unable to continue his function as city Corporation Counsel, chief adviser and political strategist to the mayor for obvious reasons. He was, in effect, exiled from the arena. This was probably the goal of the indictment in the first place. The administrative and political gap left was filled at the top in two ways by two people.

The first was Bill Lucy. As written earlier, Bill was a very smart, thoughtful, committed guy. I never got to know a lot about Bill's personal, pre Utica life, but always got the impression that he had a kind of father/son or mentor/student kind of love for Fred. I also got the impression that part of Bill thought Fred guilty of the corruption and, therefore, dirty. I thought this tore both men apart in some very deep ways. I have no way of really knowing if my feelings were correct but I did, in researching this book, read a letter from Bill to one of Fred's brothers that, at least hints that I was correct in my assumption.

The second lead in this near Greek tragedy was John Assaro. Johnny filled the power vacuum created by Fred's situation in terms of being the chief political advisor to Dick. I'll never forget the scene in the mayor's office when a bunch of us were called in to discuss Fred's fate within the administration after his acquittal. I was young and pretty stupid in grasping certain realities. I, and some others close to the throne, simply had assumed that Fred would return and that everything would go on as it did before. Someone at the meeting voiced that assumption. It wasn't me. John jumped up from the couch he was stretched out on and shouted, "If anyone thinks I'm going to give up what I have now, they're f***in' crazy!" Mayor Assaro did not say a word. The situation was perfectly clear; Fred Nassar was not going to return as he left. John had assumed his position of power and influence and he was not about to give it up.

I don't know who met with Fred after that meeting. What I do know is that Fred was given a half hearted offer to come back as Corporation Counsel but to play a diminished role in both City Hall and in Assaro politics. Anyone who knew Fred knew that he would never swallow that kind of offer. His honor needed to be restored by a full embrace by the mayor. Otherwise, one might get the impression that he really did do something wrong. I'm convinced that this is how his mind worked.

Several of us who deeply admired and respected Fred Nassar thought about threatening to resign in protest. I remember speaking to him directly about it. I should say that I remember speaking to him half heartedly about it. I was a young man with a wife and three kids. I had no money in the bank and still owed student loans. If I quit, where was I to go? And, not too deeply down was also the pure high of being close to political power. I loved the fact that people knew I had a lot of sway with the mayor. I loved the image that went with being a big political deal. Dinner at Nash's every Friday night and lunch at Grimaldi's, Basile's or Pescatores with the group was a rush to a young man infatuated with political power. This kind of feeling was not easy to walk away from, particularly for a young guy. And, others shared that feeling. I think Fred recognized all of these factors as he spoke to some of us and advised us to stay. He, of course, couched things in terms of "the city needs you," and all the public service stuff but, I think he knew that we were blowing smoke to make ourselves feel better.

My favorite movie of all time is *High Noon*. It's an allegory for standing up for what you believe in the face of danger and odds that you won't make it. It is a code many think they should live but have a hard time practicing or living up to. Most of us are not heroes or all that strong. To this day, I regret that I was not stronger for Fred Nassar. He was a visionary, a noble man who was severely mistreated by the very community he sought to help. It took me awhile to realize that I also did not stand up for myself by not quitting the administration. In straight political and administrative terms, letting Nassar go was the only correct choice. Morally, it was wrong. True friends do not desert in time of crises. Deep down, I had a bit of John Assaro in me.

With Fred gone, my influence also had to grow. The lesson that political power and ambition often trumps doing what is right was not lost on me. It is a tale often told in the history of politics but one that should be retold time and time again to new players and leaders.

The 1969 Election

In November of 1969, Dick Assaro was reelected. The election that year was a three way race between Dick, the Republican candidate Bob Lynch and a guy name Tom Carville who ran as a third candidate. Dick won with 49% of the vote. The total was about 1,000 votes less than he received two years earlier. Then as now, my political analysis said that in a Utica dominated by ethnic Italians and that the only Italian candidate had an edge that was tough to overcome. Dick also continued to benefit from his being the first Italian-American mayor.

But, I must say, we ran one hell of a campaign. Lucy played the Nassar role of directing strategy. I was also elevated to a much larger campaign role in strategy, writing, opinion, and organization. My little, very cute kids were even used in a terrific TV commercial. As the camera zoomed in on them, the voice said, "Vote Assaro, for them."

Another very interesting aspect of the campaign was our support from the Kennedy boiler room girls. They and the organizational technique they headed were first introduced to the Assaro group in the last campaign. Jerry Bruno, who was still involved with the Kennedy clan, brought in the women organizers in the spring. They were three, Esther Newburg, Mary Joe Kopechne and another young lady whose name escapes me. Kopechne was to die tragically at Chappaquiddick in the Teddy Kennedy car crash. I have heard Esther "Lobster" Newburg mentioned on the Don Imus radio show quite frequently. She is, or was, his book agent. The significant aspect of what they did in Utica was to introduce us to, and train us in, the most modern telephone based get-out-the-vote effort in those days. In the 1960s, targeted polling was in its infancy and voter efforts were handled by the political party committee system. Campaign systems built around telephone calling were unknown to a large extent and the Kennedys had the very best model. They, in effect, gave it to us. The Kennedy girls set it up, helped us work it and trained our own boiler room girls.

Another Kennedy technique we used was to stage a special and unique mayor's reception. This involved having social parties in each major section of the city, hosted by the mayor and his wife. Prior to each event, a classy invitation was sent to every Democrat in the particular section the party was covering, say East Utica, inviting the resident to spend an evening with Mayor and Mrs. Assaro. This invitation was meant to engender the belief that the receiver was special. It also served as a political mailing that the voter had in hand. The intent was that getting a personal invite from the mayor would by itself encourage or galvanize support.

The Kennedy party format was so exact that it specified what beverages were to be served: a light, non-alcoholic punch and coffee only. No beer, no hard booze. There was to be dance music of the non rock variety. "Assaro girls" would greet and register guests. The registration data would become political lists used for the get out the vote operation, volunteer recruiting and financial solicitation. At the start of the party, Mayor Assaro would welcome people, introduce his wife, make a very short political pitch and finish by telling all to have a good time. He and Penny would then circulate among the guests.

These low key social events were monitored from afar by Bruno. I was in charge of their overall organization, assisted by Joe Karam, Rock Benedetto and Buddy Gigliotti. After each of the four events, Bruno would call me for a report from wherever he happened to be. The West Utica party and what happened is an interesting observation of the Kennedy group mind set and standards.

It was to be held at the Polish Community Club on Columbia Street in the heart of West Utica. In those days, the west side was heavily ethnic Polish, my people. As we were organizing the event, the club leaders raised the question of serving beer. That

was a Kennedy no-no. So, I said no. They continued to push. How could anyone even think about inviting a room full of Poles to a party and not serve piwo? It was unheard of. Without talking to Bruno, I relented and we wound up serving the beer. The party was a tremendous success, even though quite a few Poles got drunk.

Bruno must have spoken to Dick or Johnny because when he called me late that night he was livid. How dare a young, squirt like me change the formula! He was yelling so loudly over the phone that my wife got unnerved. I kept trying to tell him how great the party was but he did not care; a Kennedy rule had been broken. That was not to be repeated. Ever. Part of me thought Bruno was over reacting. The other part realized how professional and exacting he was. He was from the big leagues of politics and did not take kindly to a minor leaguer defying him and his standards.

But, whatever we did worked as we won re-election. In winning, we overcame the aftermath of the Nassar trial and the endorsement of Bob Lynch by the Utica newspapers. Those obstacles were interrelated since the paper never seemed to accept Nassar's acquittal which was really the acquittal of the administration. At the time, it seemed we could overcome just about anything.

We were pumped and sitting on top of the world as the champagne flowed at Valley View that election night. I vividly recall a newspaper column, written soon after by *OD* reporter Ed Byrne that speculated about an Assaro dynasty. It was to be a dynasty built on brains. We were touted as having the most qualified, professional, bright staff and administration in the city's history. We were to bring modern government to Utica. We believed every word of it. Inherent in this newness was that the Rufie Elefante, political boss style of politics and government in Utica was forever defeated and gone. This was the point of the true modernization of the city, from which all else would spring.

The Dynasty, 1969-1971

Bill Lucy left the administration and the area soon after. Fred Nassar was gone as well. I think Bill left because of the Nassar scandal and his belief that something really was amiss in the administration. Perhaps he also realized that ambitions beyond Utica were not to be reached with the Assaro group. And, among some, the perception that money changing hands for political favors was growing with the growing influence of John Assaro. I think Bill was afraid of what he perceived as future trouble. And with Fred gone, Bill did not fit in very well with the type and tenor of the guys close to Dick. As mentioned earlier, Bill was a policy wonk and did not run with the crowd. You'd never see Bill at a card game, horse race or lavish dinner.

The question of how clean the Administration was merits discussion as it relates to matters as the Lucy exit. Years later I had a discussion with Tony Gaetano, Gates, as we called him. It was actually after Dick Assaro's funeral in 1980. Gates was yet another very smart guy who did fit in and ran with the gambling, good time wing of the Assaro group. He was also extremely close to Lucy. Tony left either at the same time or soon after Bill did. Both went to work for the new Syracuse mayor, Lee Alexander. As we talked of the old days, Tony mentioned that he was convinced that most of us were on the take. If he believed that, I find it hard not to believe that the issue was not discussed extensively between Lucy and him. Tony's comment reaffirms my feeling that Lucy left for this reason. I couldn't stop laughing as I related to Tony that working for Dick actually cost me money. Gates had feared the worse about rumors of political payoffs poisoning the Assaro group well.

In the years that I worked for Dick and spent a lot of time with Johnny Assaro, I never once saw any indication of anything illegal. Is that because I was shielded from certain things? I often wondered myself. But, in my opinion the tales of graft spread were much more fiction than fact. Utica would not be Utica if such matters were not wildly exaggerated. An irony of the Lucy, Gaetano to Lee Alexander move was that eventually Lee Alexander was indicted and convicted of wrongdoing. I think he actually served some jail time. The records of both Dick and John Assaro were unblemished. For years, there was speculation about John's activities. There still is nearly 50 years later. I never witnessed nor even heard of one illegal act taken by Dick or John.

For whatever reason it happened, the change was that in three short years, two legs of the *What Utica Needs* stool, Nassar and Lucy were gone. The brilliant strategist and the brilliant writer were both gone. The Assaro movement both politically and administratively would not be the same. Those two were as talented as any who ever served on the local level here. They were impossible to replace.

The New Look

Mayor Assaro had finally had it with Joe Karam and he was moved out of the mayor's office. For the next term, Dick asked me to become his Executive Assistant and shifted Joe to another office with a title of Budget Director. We had a new Public Safety Commissioner in the name of Angelo Benedetto. Lou Critelli had to return to GE and Jim Kennedy was shifted from Planning to become City Engineer. Carl Snitzer was brought over from Oneida County Planning to head the city department. At some point, I don't recall exactly when, Joe Tierno replaced Tony Gaetano in a press relations position. Joe worked for a local radio station, WTLB, which at that time (pre FM) was a big player in the market and did a great local news job. Joe actually covered the City Hall beat for the station. He was smart, very funny and immediately fit right in with the group close to the mayor.

The loss of both Fred Nassar and Bill Lucy dealt a big blow to our administrative and political capacity. It should also be mentioned that the interjection of John Assaro as a key decision maker was a step down since he had nowhere near the capacities of Nassar and Lucy. Neither did I, although I sure thought I did.

I also noticed a change in Dick. It was not a change for the better. He just did not seem as involved as he had been. The starch was taken out of him. I'll touch more on that in a coming section but I think the major part of Dick's change was conditioned by what did and didn't happen with Fred. Let's face it; an entire history of close family and personal relationships had gone out the window. This was a serious East Utica, old family loyalty existence that was violated and destroyed. Deep down, Dick had to realize what becoming mayor had wrought. I think he hated it.

The reader will notice that much of the Assaro section of this book deals with politics rather than governing. There are several reasons for this. First and foremost was the overwhelming fact that Utica was a hyper political city. The story of long term political bossism, shifting loyalties and change, national influences, intra family warfare and trying to ascertain who was figuratively screwing who dominated discussion, thought and interest more than pot holes and zoning changes. Remember, in those days crime was very low; there was no such thing as widely used drugs; the race issue was just evolving; homeowners maintained their houses with pride; and there were many good manufacturing jobs. Life in many respects was different than today as were governmental issues and concerns. It should also be mentioned again that mayoral terms were two years. You were constantly running and campaigning to hold on to the office. We were not to hold on much longer.

The Dynasty Crumbles

Dick Assaro was defeated in the election of 1971. He lost to Republican Mike Caruso. Dick lost by a little over a thousand votes in a two man race. He garnered about the same vote total he received in the 1969 election. His popularity in that sense did not rise nor fall. Here is the inside scoop. Dick lost for several important reasons. I can be a decent judge of those reasons since I played a key part in running that campaign. One reason, which was beyond anyone's control, was a huge anti incumbent feeling among the electorate due to tax increases from New York State, to Oneida County, to Utica. That year, incumbents got thrown out all over the place. A Democrat won the race for Oneida County Executive, a feat that had not happened since the job was created and has not been repeated since. We were a tax increasing administration. We grew government, signed onto expensive union contracts and padded the payroll with political jobs. The voter was angry. The reforms we did institute and programs we did undertake did not seem to materialize in any fashion that mattered that much to the average voter.

Spending was so out of control as we in City Hall did not exercise tight control of the budget. To give an example of how imprecise we were, in 1970, we cited a tax increase need of $10.66 per $1,000 of assessed property value. Why that number? We arrived at it during a major meeting in the mayor's office at which we were to give a final analysis of the upcoming budget, followed by submitting it to the Common Council and making it public. The long and the short of it was that Karam and we had no idea of what the real revenue need would be. We were grasping for sensible, close to accurate projections but getting nowhere. After hours of deliberation and arguing, I suggested that we just pick a number that we felt was close to reality and what the public would swallow. I suggested the date of the Battle of Hastings, 1066. That's a dead true story about how taxes were levied that year. I failed, as Dick' trusted assistant, to keep a close handle on Karam's conduct and performance as budget director and did not look over his shoulder as he worked with department heads. Dick made a mistake in naming Joe to that spot in the first place. Joe was, as bright as he was, was not disciplined for that job. And, I was too unseasoned to hold my post. Neither of us was monitoring spending closely enough and failed the mayor in that respect.

The second reason we lost was that the Republicans were finally smart enough to run an Italian American candidate. That enabled the splitting of the East Utica vote, which over the past two elections, Dick owned. Splitting that vote, along with dominating the very heavy Republican South Utica vote was a sound strategy.

Johnny Assaro directed the campaign for his brother. Early on, we had a poll commissioned that showed chinks in our armor. Dicks's popularity was measurably at a standstill. That meant that his likely vote percentage was hovering around 50% which translated into a tight election. We only did one survey since, as I mentioned earlier, polling was in its infancy and we had not imported a professional polling firm. I'm not sure any even existed for local elections at that time. We had structured our own poll with the help of some Utica College professors. In viewing the results, I even suggested to Dick and John that we sponsor a third straw candidate who could split the anti Assaro vote. My model to win was the previous election. Dick, John and Jerry Bruno, who was still advising us, all nixed the idea for several reasons including the one that it was basically illegal.

In certain ways, we ran the best of campaigns. Our commercials were sharp and we were well organized. The highlight of the campaign's pizzazz was the appearance by and endorsement of Dick by Mayor John Lindsay of New York City. Lindsay was a liberal Republican turned independent who was being mentioned as Presidential timber. He was tall and strikingly good looking. He was flown in by helicopter early one evening to a huge rally and

reception at the Valley View Golf Club. As the helicopter landed right on the 18th green, surrounded by thousands of cheering supporters, the event took on the aura of an invincible political sweep. Inside, Dick used the lines I had written to introduce Lindsay and brought the house down with humor. The whole event could not have gone better. I was invited to dinner with Dick and Lindsay after the rally. My impression of Lindsay was that he was not the brightest bulb in the lamp. I thought that if I was so unimpressed, how could he have been elected as mayor of the most important city in the world and how could he be even thought of as Presidential? My assessment turned out to be right, since Lindsay, his administration and political career soon imploded among scandal and failure. But boy, he sure was good looking.

The get out the vote operation we mounted at the grass roots level was, again, the boiler room model. This was based on carefully identifying what was our sure vote through phone surveys, identifying each voter contacted as yes, maybe and no, and by Election Day, only calling firm yes votes to get them out to the polls. In the bowels of our secret boiler room operation location, we had called all firm Assaro yes voters by early evening before the actual voting. The final calls had started early on Election Day and by 6 that night virtually all were reached. John Assaro was so confident of winning and winning big that after a huge argument with me, he issued the order to "call all Democrats." I fretted that we might be urging people who were not going to vote for us to get to the polls. To this day, I wonder if I was right. But, the order went out. I soon learned more of John's state of mind and level of confidence.

Almost immediately after that decision, he looked at me and asked me if I would, go for a ride with him. I said sure. He drove over to a bar on the West Side owned by Dick Smith, a lifelong Elefante political soldier. John got out of the car and asked me to stay behind and wait. Not that long after, he came back and flashed me

a huge wad of $100 bills. He said, "The Old Man gave me a few thousand and tomorrow morning I'm going to take it back to him and tell him to stick it up his ass!" The Old Man was Rufie Elefante and John had taken money from him. I sat in stunned disbelief. This guy, who we fought against so hard over the years, we were now taking money from. We had come full circle from the reformers to the corrupted. Rufie was covering his bases and we were one of them. If we won, I think John would still have kept the money. It would have been proof that the old "boss" was politically dead and that Johnny was the new one.

But, the real reason we lost was Dick Assaro himself. Dick campaigned like a tired guy who did not have much heart or fight left in him. Throughout the campaign, he simply did not seem energized or excited to do battle. My sense was, and still is, that deep down he did not want to win. The toll of the office and what he had been through was just too rough for him. He had lost his will to win. I didn't realize it then but looking back, I think Dick himself was not at peace with what we had become. In power, we had not achieved what we aspired to reach when we started in 1965.

No matter how much I had been worried about how the election would end, the reality of losing was still a near indescribable shock. I recall sitting in my car with my wife late that night crying like a baby. I could not believe it was all over. I could not believe we actually lost. The dream was over.

Tales Worth Telling

Many things happen in the halls of government and politics that are both funny and telling on various levels. One took place in our first term; the other the second. Both offer slices of insight into the city, its government and most importantly, the gentle nature of Dick Assaro himself.

One day while sitting in my Planning Department office I was summoned to the mayor's office without knowing why. Entering, I joined the mayor who had been meeting with two local attorneys, Irv Schwartz and Herb Brill. They had been briefing the mayor on a business venture they were involved in. They represented a businessman/inventor who had developed plans for a new type of gondola ski lift. Their pitch was to ask the mayor for city financial support in trade for the company they were forming to manufacture the lift in Utica. The city owned ski hill at the Parkway would serve as the testing ground for the lift and as a place to demonstrate it to future clients. The idea had a lot of sex appeal as it involved the creation of a new business and product, utilizing a city attraction. At the time, one of the functions I was performing at City Hall was that of grant coordinator. Since the city could not give money to a private company, I was called in and asked to start a search for some grant assistance. Neither the mayor nor I were skiers nor did we know a thing about ski lift technology. But, the product being pitched sure sounded great.

That meeting started the process under which we eventually received a grant from New York State that was structured to provide financial assistance to get the lift built, installed and put into operation. How we got the grant is the crux of the tale. Before I describe that, I'll add that we eventually passed the idea and proposal to Fred Nassar and a few others. They also knew nothing about skiing or technology. I recall Fred saying, "Ok, let's do it but make sure the damn thing works!"

Even in those days, the state and federal government were tying just about all programs into a benefit test for the poor and minorities. Don't forget, it was 1968 and the War on Poverty was well underway. I was presented with quite a challenge. How could I do a state grant application for money to develop a product that was tied to a sport so tilted to rich people? In other words, the

inner city, underprivileged demographic did not ski. Irv told me to create something, anything, we could submit because he had great political connections that would get an approval.

The solution became the infamous, "Skis for the Needy" program. We threw in a grant component under which we would buy ski equipment and in turn offer the equipment for free use by poor kids. We would thus introduce them to skiing and generate more people to utilize the Parkway ski area. And, the new gondola-type chair lift. I know it's hard to believe but, the state bought it and we got a big grant for the entire project.

The lift was constructed and Mayor Assaro was the special guest to take the first ride on it up the hill. Dick got on alone wearing a top coat and street shoes in the middle of winter. He got half way up the hill and the lift stopped dead. They could not restart it. It took hours for the fire department to get one of their big pieces of equipment in place to rescue Dick by ladder. Here was the mayor on the front page stuck on the hill on this white elephant lift! It never did work.

We did buy a lot of equipment for the poor kids, stuck it in a shack and advertised the program. I'm not sure one kid ever used the program. So, no lift and no needy skiers. Fred was livid and laced me and others up and down for not checking the lift out more carefully. Dick was mortified but took it more calmly than Fred.

Even then government was manipulated in ways that took advantage of a noble idea that turned unproductive and harmful; that of using public monies to engineer social change and fairness. The War on Poverty is still being fought, almost 50 years and $3 trillion later. We, as a nation, have learned nothing about the futility of throwing money away on well intentioned but ill conceived programs. I was a bureaucrat who got so carried away with a project I knew squat about I was willing to say or do

anything to get it funded. Dick Assaro was a truly big man and good friend for not firing me!

Tale two is all about sex. During our second term, a very popular Utica strip joint decided to push the envelope from partial nudity to full nudity. The club booked the notorious "Heaven Lee." Ms. Lee came to Utica on the heels of having been arrested in several other cities under various decency laws. The Utica newspaper got a hold of the booking in advance and the item became the hottest controversy to hit Utica since the mafia investigations. The mayor was being pressured by groups, including the churches to either stop the show or arrest Ms. Lee when she got on stage. Of course, a bunch of advisors, including members of the city attorney's office, convinced the mayor that we should see the show before jumping to conclusions. If Ms. Lee did not strip down to the bare bones, there would be no reason to arrest her.

So, a whole gang of us went to opening night. The club owner knew us and even gave us great seats. Heaven's complete strip was so quick; you couldn't really tell if she took it all off. So, we of course had to go back and keep going back until we could swear she was showing the goods. One night, a guy who worked in the city codes office approached our table. He had been hanging around the club for days and even got to meet and know Heaven Lee. He told us he wanted to ask her out but didn't know how. We were pretty drunk and offered advice. We suggested that he tell her he was a big deal in the administration and could arrange for her to receive the key to the city from the mayor himself. Lo and behold, two days later Heaven Lee herself pulled up and started walking toward City Hall. She was coming for the key. Word quickly spread. Dick was in his office; I, in mine, next to his. I took off for the men's room and put my feet up so no one could see me there. So, here was the hot stripper, scourge of morality, heading to the mayor to get her key. The idiot had actually given her the line!

Dick, in full view of his secretary, came out of his office and presented her with the key. He knew what she was there for since he heard us joking around with the codes guy. This says a lot about Dick. He did not panic, did not insult, or was not mean to Ms. Lee. He was a polite gentleman. No reporter heard what happened, thank God. I stayed in the men's room for two hours fearing Dick's wrath. When I got out, all he did was shake his head. Never said a word.

There is another punch line. I was in a group several years later who met Heaven Lee's booking agent by pure accident. Heaven Lee, he said, was transgendered, a man who had an operation to become a woman. That was why the final strip was so fast. I wonder if the codes guy found out that his love interest may have been a he.

Dick Assaro and What it All Meant

The last time I saw Dick Assaro, he was sitting on a couch at his house, surrounded by his kids. As soon as I got out the door I was overcome by emotion, for he was dying. Dick battled cancer for about a year before he died from it at the age of 54. After he left public office, I had kept in touch with him fairly steadily. We met for drinks, went to Vernon Downs and Saratoga, played some poker and consulted with each other. Dick went out on a limb in 1974 and was an early supporter of Hugh Carey's bid for governor. Carey won and Dick went to work for him in Albany. There were a couple of interesting aspects of the Carey connection that involved me directly. One evening during the gubernatorial transition period, Dick called and asked me if I would meet him at a restaurant in Rome. He said that he was expecting an important call from a key Carey connection concerning a job offer. He indicated he wanted my advice both before and after the call.

When we met, Dick informed me that so and so was going to call him to discuss the position of Appointments Secretary to the governor. The man calling, whose name I have forgotten, was a powerful guy who was rumored to control the docks in New York. In other words, he was connected in more ways than one. Dick wanted advice. If he was offered that job from that person, should he take it? My sense was that the job was big and powerful, meaning that Dick would be crazy not to take it. I also felt that if it was offered by the guy calling with strings attached, Dick should not touch it. Dick got the call. Evidently it was a more general discussion, a kind of feeling out with no specific job offer. Whatever transpired after, I don't know, except that Dick ultimately became a Deputy Commerce Commissioner in Albany, a very good job, but one not nearly as big as Appointments Secretary. Dick had made it clear that he would not sell his integrity for a bigger job. That, to me, was proof of his basic honesty and inner strength. That strength was soon to be tested beyond belief. He discovered he had cancer.

I don't recall how I learned of Dick's illness but I was fortunate to see him a lot during the worst part of it. He got too ill to travel to Albany and do his job. At the same time, he couldn't quit because of the state's health coverage. The cancer treatment was very costly. So, he asked me if I would do his weekly reports for him, written reports that went to the Commerce Commissioner. So, for a period of time, I would meet with him at his house on a Friday or Saturday to take some notes based on phone conversations he was having with staff and others during the week, and I would then draft a written report for him to submit. As hard to take as they were, I cherish those sessions to this day.

Dick Assaro was short in height. He battled like a giant during his illness, and for many months it was an extremely painful one. The little guy, as Joe Karam dubbed him years before, was truly a big guy, at the end, one of the biggest.

What did it all mean? Recently, I bumped into Lou Critelli, one of the Assaro originals. We talked about the old days. Lou said, "Dick deserved longer as mayor and a longer life." I'm not sure about the former but Dick certainly deserved a better deal than the hand that was ultimately dealt him.

It is so very hard to believe that the Assaro Movement lasted only four short years. Quite bluntly, nothing great was accomplished in a brick and mortar sense. We did not deliver substantial economic change or gain to the city. Perhaps the Assaro contribution is best understood with the word, pioneer. Dick has the permanent distinction of having been the city's first Italian American mayor. His election did signal the final end of boss politics, the Elefante era, by proving once and for all the Italian American in Utica could lead in an open democratic fashion. They did not require a behind the scenes only puppet master. Although Rufie Elefante continued to be a peripheral political force, the Assaro ascendancy ended Rufie's complete control of the Democratic Party in Utica even in its East Utica bastion of power. In that sense, Rufie was beaten from within. Most important, boss politics was replaced by modern government in the city of Utica.

Dick Assaro led the way for future generations of Italian American mayors. Mike Caruso, Lou LaPolla, Tim Julian, David Roefaro; they all owe a bow to the first, Dominick Assaro.

To this day, the Assaro administration is still remembered as the one "with all the brains." We did put together one which was by far the most advanced and qualified in the history of the city, bar none, before and after. Did that matter? Sadly, the answer is no. Our major accomplishments from a policy and programmatic point of view were basically two. We were successful in expanding the stalled downtown Urban Renewal development project, by expanding its boundaries onto Genesee Street the city's primary retail corridor, which made way for what is now the Radisson Hotel complex. In order to accomplish that, we had to incorporate the Kennedy Plaza public housing complex, which was then built by the New York State Urban Development Corporation. This change in project boundaries took a long time to accomplish and was to signal a downtown revival. That revival never fully occurred and is an issue to this day, nearly 40 years later. Our second achievement was the alteration of the old Parkway to the new one-way street traffic pattern under what was then called the TOPICS Program. The system better serves the city and its traffic pattern to this day. In the scheme of things, these were modest accomplishments.

But, all the fancy talent we brought in did not mean all that much to the average Utican. The taxpayer wants the basics, safety, clean streets, and parks for the kids and the trash picked up on time. Things like urban renewal, so called job creation strategies, downtown master plans and the like are only things editorial writers and bureaucrats think are important. All of our brain power did not light the fire of aspiration for excellence in Utica. We either did not know how or it couldn't be done. Short election cycles do not afford the time for dreamers. Fred Nassar was right in his dictum to embrace and push the immediate. Ironically, that was also Rufie Elefante's belief. He had a decades long career helped by building at least one election year showcase building his mayors could point in a campaign. That was more effective politically than all of our model city fantasies. In that sense Fred and Rufie were on the same page.

Significant change and progress to places like Utica can only come from the outside. In this sense, the Assaro story is one of the might have been. Big, powerful, national and state political connections were needed to do big things. A Bobby Kennedy presidency might have brought the major north-south highway connection that would link the Utica area with Canada and the southern tier. Would a Kennedy or a Humphrey presidency have brought a major engineering/scientific university to inner Utica that would have tied into RADC at Griffiss and spurred tremendous levels of research dollars and scientists into the area? Would this have led to spin offs of new industry creating thousands of jobs. Would that have meant the expansion of a GE and other defense industries?

Utica and the area were put on the national political map through the Assaro movement. An assassination and a presidential election lost by a whisker knocked us off that map. I'll close this section with a story. Hubert Humphrey was again elected to the Senate from Minnesota in 1970. He gladly consented to do an endorsement TV commercial for Dick's race. Dick, Joe Karam and I went to Washington, D.C. to film it. We did the shot at Humphrey's Watergate apartment. HHH was as warm and friendly of a guy one could ever meet. Finally, as we were leaving, the last image I recall was one of the Happy Warrior hugging Dick. Humphrey never did forget what Utica meant to him in 1968! My thought then and now, is what would it have meant to Utica if that man was elected President?

That pretty much sums up the Assaro period of being one of, what ifs and unfulfilled opportunities for the city and the Assaro group. But, what a ride it was!

Personal Transition

When it was all over, I was 28 years old, married, father of three and broke. I had finished five of the most exciting years of life that a young man could imagine. I had met Kennedy, Humphrey, Muskie, Lindsay and McGovern. I had nothing to show for it and was job hunting. My ego was trashed and I was afraid of an unknown future.

As I look back, I wonder why, at the time, I limited my job search to the public sector. It would have been a perfect time to dump politics and government and hit the private sector. But in those days there were no job consultants, head hunters and the like. So, I limited myself. I received a job offer from the mayor of Jacksonville, Florida. I clearly recall my trip there and the interview. In the cab ride from the airport to the city hall, the cab driver was giving me a brief view of the city. I had been to a conference there once with Dick but we didn't see much of the city. Much of what came out of the cabby's mouth referred to the n*****s". Being a Northerner, coming from an integrated high school, playing sports with many blacks, some of whom I loved as brothers, I was stunned, embarrassed and angry to be in that cab. The Deep South in 1971 was indeed foreign. But, I liked the mayor and his chief assistant very much. I thought the interview went well. But, on the way home, I was really antsy about the prospect of a move.

The interview did go well because a few days later I received a job offer. I asked the mayor if I could have a few days to think it over and discuss things with my wife. He granted my request. Since I had no money, a house to sell and no wherewithal to handle a huge move with a family, I was scared out of my mind. Just before I was to go ask my in-laws for some moving help, the phone rang and Bill Valentine was on the line. Valentine was the mayor of Rome, NY. I had known him since high school through sports and he, Dick Assaro and I had gotten along very well when both of them were mayors of the neighboring cities. Valentine asked if I was interested in discussing coming to work for him. I told him, I'd be right up to talk about it. In a few weeks, I was in my car to start my first day as the Planning Director of the City of Rome. I was about to start the second phase of my professional career in a close but very different place.

Chapter Two
Bill Valentine's Rome—1971-1979

I drove into Rome on the morning of February 11, 1972 with two thoughts. I was relieved that I was able to find a job in the area. And two, we could avoid moving to Jacksonville. I did, however, view becoming Rome's Director of Planning compared to serving as the chief assistant to Utica's mayor as being comparable to being sent down from the majors to the minors. Uticans had always viewed Rome as a small town that primarily served as a hiding place to cheat on wives or girlfriends. My personal experience with the city was limited to coming in and out for basketball and baseball games and an occasional trip as a kid to air shows at Griffiss Air Force Base.

At the time I arrived on the scene, Rome was a city of about 52,000, roughly half the size of Utica. Economically it was dominated by Griffiss Air Force Base, a Strategic Air Command (SAC) base that employed over 8,000 people with an annual payroll of $80 million. Within the Base was RADC, the Rome Air Defense Center, one of the Air Force's top scientific research facilities. RADC employed some 1,200 people with a very high annual payroll given the high tech nature of its jobs. Griffiss was a huge regional employer only rivaled by General Electric in Utica. Other major employers were Revere Copper and Brass and Rome Strip Steel. Commercially, Rome was woefully under served, losing a ton of shopping dollars to both Syracuse and Utica.

This story of Rome starts and ends with its mayor from 1964 to 1980, William Valentine. Under Bill Valentine's leadership, Rome was attempting to remake itself in several substantial ways. It was in the midst of a major downtown Urban Renewal project complete with the reconstruction of Fort Stanwix, an important Revolutionary War era fort. It was also involved in a big project to restore a section of the old Erie Canal and to create a canal village. The first shovel of dirt turned to construct the original canal has taken place in 1817. Both the fort and canal were significant to the nation and to Rome.

The city was attempting to diversify its economy by expanding its local commercial base and by becoming a tourist destination. The plans and programs of Rome were exciting to me and I soon embraced being a part of the effort. I quickly grasped that there was a heck of a lot more redevelopment going on in Rome than we had planned or initiated in Utica.

What was also very apparent nearly from day one, were the political differences between the two cities of Oneida County. In Utica, political concerns and battles seemed to take place daily; they were almost completely absent in Rome. Looking back on it, I attribute the difference to two factors. First, the mayor's term of office was four years as compared to two in Utica. Second was Bill Valentine himself.

The Mayor, City and Its Government

Bill Valentine was a tall, imposing former Niagara University basketball star who also spent years refereeing and coaching. He refereed many of my high school basketball games when I played at Utica Free Academy in the late 1950s and 1960. He was an ex jock who loved sports, particularly basketball all his life. He was also noted to be fair, honest and direct. He lived modestly, was a strong family man and looked after those who worked with him as if they were an extended family. The strength of his personality and character led to an extremely high level of political popularity. Electorally in Rome he was virtually unbeatable.

As a result, he was not seriously challenged in the four mayoral elections in which he ran. He pretty much had his own way with the city's Common Council as well. The council in Rome was much more at ease, cooperative and willing to compromise than the Utica council. I think the members knew Valentine was stronger and more popular. They also seemed more civic oriented as opposed to the politically driven council of Utica. To understand why, one had to grasp a couple of the basics about Rome.

Rome was more educated and more cosmopolitan than Utica. I quickly learned that far from feeling inferior to the larger Utica and its people, Romans viewed Uticans as dumber, more corrupt and self destructive. The average Roman felt superior to the average Utica resident. I think there were three basic reasons why.

The Air Force base brought in new people on a constant basis. That included both military and the civilians representing companies who did work on base. As a result, more Romans had seen other parts of the country and the world. They had a broader view.

Rome also had no history of crime and political scandal. There was no boss in Rome a la Rufie Elefante. Through the years, Utica became nationally referred to as Sin City and Little Chicago; Rome's reputation was pristine. Rome had no national image but had a self image of being squeaky clean.

Rome had several strong family owned companies whose owners and leaders viewed the community and their roles in it much differently than Utica's business community. Rome Strip Steel, Rome Iron and several other metals related industries were large employers. In Utica, the knitting mill industry that so dominated the city pre-WWII had left for the south and were replaced by national companies such as GE and Bendix who were not headquartered in Utica. Their executives and managers moved in and out. They viewed their civic participation and responsibilities differently. Rome's industrial ownership base was home grown and lasting. In 1974, the Utica newspaper wondered aloud editorially why Rome was able to accomplish so much more than the larger Utica. These were some of the answers to that question.

I quickly established a terrific relationship with Mayor Valentine. We were both early to work guys. Every morning, I'd come in an hour early and find him already at his desk ready to talk sports and politics, two topics he loved. He was completely square. He didn't swear at all. Didn't talk about women except an occasional reference to his wife Hazel and didn't complain about others. In the seven years that I saw him almost daily, I only heard him say a bad word about two people, George Waters and Carl Eilenberg. Bill didn't like either of them largely because of their sniping. Waters through a column he wrote as publisher of the *Rome Daily Sentinel*, the city's daily newspaper, and Eilenberg from his radio show were frequent Valentine critics. Valentine viewed them as pompous and condescending.

The mayor's top aide and confidant was Dick Fahy, who was City Treasurer. Dick was also a jock, a very good basketball player in his day at Utica College and as straight a shooter in the broader sense of the word as you'd ever want to meet. The mayor did not make a move or a decision without hearing from Fahy. Dick was a de facto Valentine family member minus the blood connection. The mayor also had a "kitchen" cabinet of outsiders with whom he called in for consultation on most key issues. They included a local attorney, Jack Grow, and Bob Rosenberg, a businessman who was also President of the Common Council, and another business guy named Don McLaughlin. All of these men were the leaders within the city's Republican Party.

Unlike Utica, in which the Democratic Party was split into factions, and as a result never fully supported Dick Assaro, the tie between the Rome mayor and the city Republican Party was strong and unified. This lessened conflict over issues and major decisions to a very large extent. Valentine had the same rule as Assaro; say anything to me behind the closed door of my office, but when the door opens, we speak as one. This applied to staff and political allies. The unified Republican Party structure offered a well ordered process that was heaven compared to the hell of fragmented politics in Utica. It is important to note that I entered the Rome scene in Valentine's third, four year term. He had already been in office for eight years. Dick Assaro had but four. The continuity factor alone accounted for many of the administrative and political differences of the two cities and their mayors.

Valentine's secret weapons were a reporter named Ernie Gray and the mayor's son, Mike. Gray covered the City Hall beat for the *Daily Sentinel*. He and the mayor were comfortable with each other and respected each other's views. The person who walked into the office daily about a half hour after I got there was Gray. He had special full access to the mayor and the mayor picked Ernie's brain as well. I could not imagine a relationship as this between a Utica mayor and a reporter from the Utica newspaper. Gray, in his articles tilted for Valentine's positions and he also wrote a weekly column that often viewed Valentine, his policies and staff in a favorable light. His top boss, Waters may have been a critic but he did give Ernie free reign. Mike Valentine was a businessman who worked for a Utica based company and was very smart. Mike and Dick Fahy were also close friends. I sensed that although the mayor's son was rarely seen in City Hall, everything of importance was bounced off of him. Given Mike's business background and good sense, he was a key and valuable advisor to his dad.

Another feature of the administration involved the city attorneys. In the seven years I worked for Bill Valentine, he had two, Frank Cook and Dave Grow. Grow succeeded Cook. Both were young, smart and extremely blunt and honest. Most important, they were

Corporation Counsels who found ways to get things done once the mayor made decisions. This emphasis on positive, aggressive implementation by asking how we can do it, as opposed to why we can't do it, was very similar to the Nassar style when Assaro started in Utica. The importance of having a results oriented city attorney cannot be minimized in municipal government

The Congressional Decision

I started to crack into the inner sanctum of the mayor's office soon after I arrived. Interestingly, it was a political issue that first called me in. Al Pirnie, the long time Republican Congressman from Utica and New Hartford, announced that he was retiring. Pirnie was an outstanding man, very popular and pretty powerful and well liked on the Republican side of the aisle in Washington. I had had the pleasure of knowing him at least superficially. I went to grade school with his son, Doug, and as Utica College Young Republican Club President, I helped in Pirnie's campaign one year. Most critically for Rome and the entire area, he was a member of the powerful House Armed Services Committee. His seat on this committee was considered by most to be all important to the preservation of Griffiss Air Force Base and its tremendous economic influence on the area and city.

A bunch of local Republicans wanted Pirnie's job. They included his main assistant, Sherwood Boehlert, Vin DiOrio, a top Republican attorney out of Utica who was the power behind the throne of Utica Mayor Mike Caruso, another Utica attorney and New York State Assemblyman John Buckley, and a Herkimer County based state senator, Don Mitchell. Many Republicans both from Rome and outside the region thought that Bill Valentine would be the best candidate of all if he could be persuaded to jump in. He was popular wherever he went, would have a lock on the block of votes from Rome and the western part of the district, and had the most knowledge of the Griffiss AFB, the most important facility in the district. His stature as a sports figure aided his contacts and popularity throughout the region. The bottom line was that everyone liked Bill and he might be the only one who could unite the fragmented Party with its group of candidates. Valentine was also a very popular Italian-American figure in Utica. This was due to his sports background and to the good press he got in the Observer Dispatch.

Mayor Valentine seriously considered taking the plunge. I was asked to participate in a series of meetings in his office to discuss the matter. I was looked to for advice because I knew Utica area politics and its political actors. It was both fun and telling. As we analyzed the race, several of us felt that Valentine could and would win the Republican primary. And, that meant winning the general election. The district, which comprised Oneida, Herkimer counties, and parts of counties north and southeast to include Cooperstown and Oneonta, was then so overloaded with registered Republicans that a dead guy on that line would probably win. Valentine felt he could win the primary if he jumped in as the unifying candidate.

After a brief cat and mouse game in the media, he decided not to enter the race. To understand the decision, you had to understand Bill Valentine. He was a man comfortable in his own skin and that skin included his "town" and his family. He could not picture himself away from either. He was also not a financially well off guy and I think knew D.C. well enough to know that it would have been a tough financial deal, especially for the first couple of terms. Finally, as he said it, he was not a back slapping kind of guy and did not like to raise money. Given the low key of politics in Rome and the lack of big political issues, he had no reason to play political games or to raise a lot of political money. I sensed he knew that the games congressmen had to play were that they were not for him. All the candidates courted him for an endorsement but he remained neutral. Don Mitchell won and succeeded Al Pirnie. The others split the Oneida County primary vote while the

Herkimer County area united solidly behind Mitchell. Most important, particularly from a Rome outlook, was that Mitchell was able to retain the seat on the Armed Services Committee. This seat was vital to keeping the Base in Rome.

That was really the only big, straight political issue that arose during my seven years working for Valentine. To me, this was a blessing given the raw taste Utica politics had left in my mouth. My job and the many exciting challenges I got involved with in Rome were all professional in the sense of municipal and community work. Unlike Utica where everything seemed to be political, in Rome, not much was.

Some Characteristics and Differences

This absence of politics played a big role in the Valentine administration's ability to control cost and taxes. One of the amazing accomplishments of the Valentine era was that taxes, over a 16 year period did not increase in real dollars. Mayor Valentine was proud to point out that city taxes under his leadership were actually less than they were when he started. How many mayors could have made this claim? Valentine was able to for two primary reasons mentioned earlier; the strong financial control of the budgets exercised and monitored by Dick Fahy and the lack of the need to create jobs for political purposes.

There was also a huge cultural difference within the City Halls. In contrast to Utica, there was no swearing, no gambling, carousing in Valentine's group. It was relaxed but totally clean and as they used to say, square. The Rome mayor did not smoke and hardly had a drink. In Utica, as described in the last chapter, wine, women and song laced with strong language and gambling was the norm. The two most in charge of Rome's government, Valentine and right hand man Fahy, were strong Catholics. Both were products of Catholic schools and both devoted family men. Dick's only vices included beer and cigarettes. Neither was unusual then. Will, as the mayor was called by some of his close friends did not smoke and had a very occasional glass of wine. In the seven plus years I worked with them I never heard a word about things like gambling or women. Other differences were also clear.

In Rome, there was no overload of city employees. There were no layers of bureaucrats falling over one another. No fancy titles. One person did the jobs of two, rather than two doing the job of one. Although this is jumping ahead of the story, another example of how the cost of government was viewed and handled was illustrated in what was called the community development arena. In the mid 1970s the federal government created the Community Development Block Grant program. Under this program, cities were given money grants to carry out federally defined development activities. When this program was instituted in Rome, the mayor named me to handle its administration. We ran it with a bare bones staff of existing Planning Department personnel and one program assistant. Virtually all program activities went for things like street paving and playground improvements in city neighborhoods. The strategy we had was to use the federal money as substitute for city money on projects that the city would have had to abandon. This is how we saved money, minimized expense and city budget growth.

To this day, many cities use these federal dollars to create vast layers of employees and special programs. In 2007, I accepted an offer from the then mayor of Utica to work for him and budget and development matters, more of which follows in a later chapter. But one thing I found was a development office bureaucracy that was loaded with people falling all over each other, most not working a full day and most working on things that were completely non essential to the well being of the city. For example, there was a position funded to the tune of well over $50,000 a year, including benefits, for a person whose sole job was pretty much to film TV shows for the mayor! I often kidded both this guy and the mayor about the twenty or so people who actually watched the show. Other activities went to granting gifts to certain groups like senior centers and other activities designed to ingratiate the administration with voting blocks. Many jobs were held for strictly political purposes and those holding them were barely up to even paper shuffling. I was staggered by the hundreds of thousands of dollars needlessly spent on "administration" while city neighborhoods literally burned. I realize that federal regulations changed along with the advent of the politically correct culture of promoting mumbo jumbo and calling it government service, but I often wondered how much better all would be if the Utica operation in the 2000s were run as Rome's was in the 1970s.

As I now think about and illustrate differences, modern politicians and administrators will probably think that the old days had it backwards and all of the feel good activities and jobs that go with them are not only important but good for a community. I say look around at your neighborhoods and your tax rates. Valentine and Fahy understood what was most important, controlling taxes. There were many events and issues that tell the Rome story during the Valentine years. I will tell the most important.

They were important to the development of the city and in some instances reached beyond its boundaries. Some involved personalities that shaped both local and state history.

The Nu Way Revisited

In the late 1950s, early 1960s, smart business people realized that a modern north-south highway connection would be a major plus to the economic development of the Utica-Rome area. Much as the Thruway created an efficient east-west transportation network for commerce, a north-south route linking the area with Canada to the north and Binghamton to the south was essential to accommodate truck shipping into and out of the area. Its availability would serve as a magnet to new industry dependent upon the transport of goods. The model of this premise was Route 81 through Syracuse.

The Route 81 story is among the many "if only" stories that have dominated the folklore of the Utica-Rome area since the 1950s. This and other examples, some true, some not, have given our citizens something to blame and grumble about for all of those decades. It's like the baseball player who thinks he could have made "the show" if only seen by the right scout. The political story of how Syracuse landed Route 81 in the first place also contributed to the inferiority complex and jealousy of Syracuse among the locals. So, we wanted ours since Syracuse got its super highway.

Efforts to land this highway connection had failed through several attempts and several governors over the years. In early 1972, a new business group was formed to revive the effort to lobby and convince New York State to commit vast resources to this project. The name Nu Way was originally used to describe the highway plan but was dropped by the new group. The effort reawakened in a much more low key, less public way than past efforts. The business group, headed by a Utica businessman Peter Carparelli, decided to include only one elected official to lead the effort and that was Bill Valentine. Since Nelson Rockefeller was governor, the group felt a Republican politician was necessary to its success. At that time, the Oneida County Executive was Democrat Bill Bryant, and Mike Caruso was the anything but influential Republican Mayor of Utica.

Valentine was perceived to have a number of strengths. He had been in office for a long time, had stature within both his political party and state government groups like the New York State Conference of Mayors and most of all, and could be trusted to keep the effort beneath the public radar screen. Anyone who knew anything about Nelson Rockefeller immediately knew he hated attempts at public pressure and would kill the effort if that was tried. Valentine agreed to help and asked that I provide the staff support to the committee. It was agreed.

The strategy was pretty simple. We would secure a meeting with the governor at which we would make the request that he direct the state Department of Transportation to seriously study the proposal, based on the compelling economic justification presented to the governor at that meeting. The trick was to secure a meeting. Our group felt that if Rockefeller agreed to a meeting that alone would signal that he was open to the project. Most of us thought that we would not be successful in landing the meeting but that we should make the attempt anyway. We would not do any work building a case unless and until we had the meeting commitment with Rockefeller himself.

It came as a shock to me when the Governor agreed to meet with us. I had expected to be shunted off to staff. Perhaps we did indeed have a shot. That meant that we had to create and offer a dynamite presentation that would move the project forward. Our mission was to create a compelling case at the meeting to interest Rocky to unleash his influence and office to help push the project. We knew that without the governor's support, we would be wasting our time.

As I recall, the meeting date given to us meant that we had to do a lot of preparation in a short period of time. The first decision made was to keep small the group going to the meeting. It was to include Carparelli, Valentine, the person in charge of making the presentation and me. A very nice, successful, local Republican businessman on the committee was designated to give the presentation. This man, who was not a well known public figure, was very sincere, but surprisingly inexperienced in being involved in a presentation of this nature.

I marshaled some professional staff people to put the presentation together and to work with the presenter on his delivery. The presentation itself turned out to be a pretty straight but long economic impact approach that projected significant economic growth if the transportation route became a reality. We worked long hours both day and night to get it done on time. It turned out to be pretty convincing and surprisingly good for being done in such a rush. The benefits to our area and to the state were substantial. We were excited at our opportunity and very hopeful of success.

The fellow doing the presentation got more nervous by the day, the hour, the minute, as the meeting day approached. He kept calling and calling, wondering aloud over our product and his ability to sell it. I kept telling him not to worry but to just treat it like he was closing a big business sale which he had frequently done in his business career.

D-Day arrived and we piled into one car and headed to Albany to meet with Rocky. We were in good spirits, and discussed how we were going to handle things after the meeting. Our thinking was that we would have a lot more work to do once the governor was on board. We were assuming the governor would be receptive to supporting moving ahead. Why else would he meet?

When we arrived at the State Capitol Building, we were met and ushered into a huge meeting room with a very large ornate, heavy wooden table. We got situated before any sign of Rockefeller. We had our big presentation booklet ready.

After a fairly long wait, Rockefeller walked in with a pretty big entourage and sat down in the middle of the table facing us. Immediately after sitting down, he looked up and said in typical Rockefeller fashion, "You can't have your highway, it's too much money! What else can I do for you, fellas?" We were stunned, deflated and confused all at once. We didn't get the chance to say one word and we were shot down. I can't even remember what we said or didn't say after that. It didn't matter. Meeting over and done. Just like that. Highway gone.

I don't think two words were spoken all the way home. The businessman, who did not get to give his presentation, was as white as a ghost. I often wondered whether he was more relieved by not giving it than disappointed not to get his place in the Rockefeller sun.

I tell this story for two reasons. First, this is yet another example of the area not being able to be on the receiving end of a significant intergovernmental commitment that could have permanently changed the future of the area. As was the inability to land the dream of a State University offering engineering degrees, the inability to get a north-south highway connection added to the list of examples of the lack of clout the area had to achieve big projects that could lead to exciting, new growth and expansion.

The other reason is to give the reader the flavor of Nelson Rockefeller. In my life, I have met high level politicians of all stripes; a President, three Vice Presidents, several governors, a few candidates for President. Only a couple made the hair on the back of my neck stand up. One was Nelson Rockefeller. His presence in a room was all commanding. It was not his size, since he was not very big, but he simply overpowered the room and all in it. He oozed power and self confidence. I was blown away at his just looking at us and simply saying a loud no. He was the boss, in control and that was it. I guess all that money helped but I also think the breeding that he had, more unique than most, stood him above the crowd. To this day, I find it stunning that given his ability and money he was not able to become President of the United States. I'll bet it drove him nuts as well.

War for Survival

On January 21, 1974, the United States Air Force declared war on Rome and the rest of central New York. In August, 1975, the Air Force surrendered. This war story tells a lot about the area, its politics and its expectations that continue to affect what we are and, what we realistically hope to be.

The Air Force announced on that fateful day that it was splitting the Rome Air Defense Center and relocating its missions to bases and labs in other parts of the country. As previously mentioned, RADC was a top scientific mission that had a major socio-economic impact on the entire region. It was critical to the well being of Rome in particular. RADC at the time employed 1,435 people: 1,119 civilian and 316 military. Its annual payroll was $45 million, by far the largest payroll generator in the area. That average annual salary of $41,000 per person in 1974 illustrates the nature of the scientific jobs and advanced capabilities of the RADC work force. This was, in short, the crème de la crème of Rome and the area. It was obvious to even the casual observer that losing RADC would be a tremendous blow to the community.

In less than 24 hours after the announcement, the community, its leaders, and most critically many of those working directly and indirectly for RADC decided to fight back. Bill Valentine publically issued a call to arms to reverse the Air Force's decision. The first step the mayor took was to charge me with putting together a quick but comprehensive white paper on the impact the decision would have on Rome. Neither he nor I fully understood how important this would be. Congressional rules specified that decisions of this nature not bring economic devastation to communities. These types of laws were installed as a mechanism to help protect congressmen from the kinds of military decisions that could cost representatives their seats.

I immediately got to work with my one staff guy, Paul Wilde and Dick Fahy from within City Hall. We reached out to many people and agencies for help in providing data. We and many others dropped everything else and worked long hours to get the job done. The report was completed in a matter of days. It was submitted to the mayor who released it for public consumption.

It concluded that, "If the nation is in the midst of a recession, Rome will be in a deep depression if this decision is implemented." The report went on to urge, "The marshalling of all necessary forces to stop the move." Of course a chimp could have figured that losing RADC would be disastrous but showing its impact in black and white did have advantages to waking up the community across the board. It also quickly armed Congressman Don Mitchell with ammunition that he could use to rally congressional support, executive branch sympathy and to submit to the Air Force.

Don Mitchell was a relatively new congressman who was still in the process of building political power and influence. Congress was heavily Democratic and the Watergate embroiled Nixon was President. Gerald Ford, an ex-congressman, was Vice President. As noted before, Mitchell inherited Al Pirnie's seat on the powerful Armed Services Committee. It was a surprise to some that the Air Force would make this decision in light of him being on that committee. But he was young and new, and that committee was dominated by Democrats whose areas would be receiving the benefits of the move.

It is interesting to note connection with the first section of this book and the role the loss of ROAMA had in Fred Nassar's recognition that the area had to build a much more influential political power base to keep and grow its economy. Here we were, not 10 years after Nassar's concern and the birth of the Assaro group facing another devastating economic loss that was politically related.

The most important step taken as the area moved into battle mode was the designation of the Joint Utica-Rome Committee on Griffiss Air Force Base to coordinate the broad effort to reverse the decision. The committee was headed by a guy named Terry Prossner. It was part of the Rome Chamber of Commerce's structure designed to handle Griffiss matters. I view this as critical because this was not a politically controlled group but one comprised of business professionals, largely from the ranks of tech reps, people working for companies that did business with the Air Force. These people knew the ins and outs of the base, the Air Force and the Pentagon. This also meant that no one politician would be grandstanding during this effort.

Speaking of politicians, it must be noted on how certain factions and personalities came together in an effective and unified way. One was Oneida County Executive Bill Bryant, who was a political rebel who marched to his own beat. Some questioned his volatility and stability. He was to leave his job later under some strange circumstances. I myself did not like or get along with him. I also knew he did not have a very positive view of me. But Bryant played a positive role in the task to save RADC in a couple of ways. First, he assigned any county agency necessary to help in the task. Second, and most important, he tried to enlist the support of fellow Democratic politicians from across the state, including powerful downstate Democratic congressmen to support our area's effort. Although I was always uncomfortable with him and didn't like him personally, I did admire his rising to the occasion as he did.

The battle to save RADC was being waged on three fronts. The first was to build on the earlier work done illustrating community impact. The second was to measure the impact of the relocations on RADC itself. Here is where the tech rep element of Prossner and a whole crew he put together came into play to show how the moves may in fact weaken Air Force research capability. This effort was inside and technical. The inside not only meant the tech rep insiders but the insiders who worked for RADC who clandestinely fed info to the Prossner group. The bottom line of this effort was making the case that many key RADC employees might not move, thus costing the Air Force valuable scientific talent. The third front was political and what Don Mitchell could do in the corridors of Congress and in White House offices. On the latter, the Watergate mess was dominating everything within the Nixon White House and the Nixon people couldn't care less about one mission at one Air Force Base in one little town.

The first crack in the Air Force's armor came in November. The Air Force announced that it would restudy its decision and hired an independent group, the Battelle Memorial Institute to do the study. Battelle was and still is one of the world's largest sciences and technology related firms that did and does defense/military/security type work. They hire the best and the brightest. It was understood that Battelle would never be hired unless the Air Force was willing to abide by the results of this, independent study. We locals wondered whether or not the study would be rigged. We feared that because Battelle did a lot of work with the military, it would simply rubber stamp what the generals wanted to do.

My contact with Battelle was interesting, enlightening and kind of funny. I was assigned the task of hosting the research team that would be coming in from Columbus, Ohio to do the community impact section of the study. They would do an objective, independent analysis separate from what we had done locally. We weren't very afraid of that part of the inquiry since the loss of the magnitude of RADC on a relatively small area was a no brainer. But what happens in these matters is that adjustment assessments can be done to illustrate that an area could recover and eventually prosper in adjusting from military to civilian. Battelle would have carte blanche to fool around with that part of the equation and perhaps knock the skids out of our disaster scenario.

I don't recall the exact number of Battelle guys who came in; it was at least four. They were young, smart, very nice, two fisted drinkers and skirt chasers. Paul Wilde and I struck up a quick friendship with them. We took them out every night, shot pool, drank beer and directed them to hot night spots in Utica. We had a great time together. I sensed that there was no way they were ever going to issue a report that would harm our cause. I was right. The impact section of their report in fact showed economic harm substantially deeper than what we had been claiming!

Before the Battelle study was started, the *New York Times* sent a reporter to investigate and report on the community angle of the controversy. I don't recall his name. He was a young, black reporter who had some role in the *Times'* Watergate reporting. He started his interviewing with us because had a copy of our impact report. As it turned out, his entire story was written in the back room of a popular Rome bar and restaurant called Coal Yard Charlie's. He also became a beer drinking buddy and he basically took all we had written and worked his story from there. He left in a few days. His *Times* story could not have been more sympathetic to us! This national coverage was noticed in the political arena beyond Rome and the area.

Who knows to what extent our socializing and schmoozing helped the cause? What it does show is that establishing personal relationships under the right circumstances are sometimes as important as details and facts. Most successful people understand this basic feature of human interaction. This sounds obvious and simplistic but many of those who serve decision makers on all levels either do not grasp this basic fact or choose to ignore it. It is often the case that the singer is more important than the song.

The full Battelle study concluded that if carried out, relocating RADC would, "devastate the local economy and result in the loss of key scientists to the Air Force." The Air Force, even in light of the study, did not reverse itself until a special Air Force panel took yet another look and concluded that, "It would be in the national interest to leave RADC in Rome." On August 1, 1975, the decision was reversed. Rome was saved!

One story about who saved RADC that has kicked around since then is that Don Mitchell convinced President Gerald Ford to order the reversal. Although the reversal actually came before Ford became President, the Vice President is not chopped liver in these matters. This is particularly true given Ford's leadership background in the House of Representatives. I don't know if the Ford story is true and Mitchell never publically confirmed it.

Who Really Won?

It should be noted that RADC, now, called Rome Labs, was saved but not grown. As this book is being written employment at what used to be RADC is about 600, less than half of what it was in 1975. In addition, the Air Force flying missions are gone and the base closed in 1995. The impact of this highly advanced scientific brain trust within our community has been severely diminished after all, along with the thousands of other military and civilian jobs generated by the other missions hosted at Griffiss. Some reasons that contributed to these losses will be discussed later in the book.

Urban Renewal

One can't write about the Rome of the Valentine era without writing about the city's attempt at remaking its downtown utilizing the old federal Urban Renewal program as a prime funding source. The story of Rome's downtown renewal efforts is an important part of the city's modern history. It also relates to differences with Utica and other cities that undertook similar efforts under the federal Urban Renewal Program. Many cities looked to that program for downtown salvation

Washington's answer to the question of how to preserve, maintain and grow our urban centers in the 1950s through the 1970s was the Urban Renewal Program. It offered healthy sums of federal money to physically redo and remake downtowns. This effort was designed to counter the flight of commercial activity to the suburbs, limit sprawl, and to keep people living, shopping and transacting business in our city centers. It was the romance of Saturday morning trips downtown with Mom or Dad in the 1940s and 1950s that captured the imagination of bureaucrat, political representative and citizen. The program was built on the belief that certain types of shoppers and merchants could be deterred from leaving cities through the modernization of roads, buildings and other aspects of inner city public infrastructure. This program was not to be the first or last time the federal government tried to fight against the tide of the urges of its own population by using tax dollars in an attempt to turn the clock back as opposed to accepting and planning around a changing future.

Although there were exceptions, in most places in the country, the Urban Renewal program was a colossal failure and waste of a lot of taxpayer money. This was particularly true in smaller cities. That should have been an early and lasting lesson in the belief that government can force feed people or business to fit into some centralized planning ideal dreamed up in Washington. But, to this day, to the great detriment of our wallets and national debt, we have not learned this lesson. We now have a federal government that is repeating the mistakes of the past. Program names have been changed, price tags have risen, but the results will be the same. The fact is that the centralized planning to direct and manage socio-economic activities simply has not, nor will not, work.

In the case of Urban Renewal, there were major flaws that the program could never overcome. Those of us on the local level were the guinea pigs that could not or did not want to grasp these flaws. The first flaw was that plans were created in and by the public sector without the consultation and involvement of an adequate level of private sector developers. Looking back, I think the reason for this was that major private developers representing major retailers had already determined that the development goal was the suburb, not the city. If this was recognized and acknowledged by politicians and planners in Washington, the program would have not been created in the first place.

The second flaw was the disregard of the basic concept of time. By that I mean the long period of time it took to create and implement an urban renewal plan and program. Consultants were hired to draw up plans, these plans had to pass through layers of public and governmental approval, property had to be acquired which involved negotiations and often legal condemnations, contracts for infrastructure meaning parking facilities, roads, utilities and the like, infrastructure had to then be built.

The last step was to actually realize the construction of the commercial, residential and/or industrial use itself. This full process took many years. That made it virtually impossible to work with a developer or business interest whether they are a big national chain or a local office builder. Market and financial conditions change in far shorter periods of time that the urban renewal process took. What most cities wound up with was a "build it and they will come" shell. In other words they lands sites and then went out to market them. This flew in the face of an actual private development process in which the end user is involved in selecting defining and creating the space in the first place under an efficient, tight schedule. Local governments that urban renewal installed in place of private sector developers were simply not prepared to do the job.

When I arrived on the scene, Rome had already adopted and started to implement its Urban Renewal plan. Getting projects built under that basic plan, was to be part of my job as Planning Director and eventually as Director of Community Development. Thirty seven years later, that job in Rome is still not done! That is the bottom line story of a project that started under the Valentine era and never ended. There are some key events that took place that partially explain what did and didn't happen. They are important to relate here because revisionist history in Rome has clouded the accuracy of what really went on. But, the bottom line is that because of the competency and diligence of the Valentine team, Rome's urban renewal effort fared much better than most. What did and didn't happen in the post Valentine era has to be answered by others who succeeded Valentine in assuming the mantle of leadership.

Prior to Urban Renewal, Rome's downtown could be characterized in three ways, old, falling apart and split. The split part was interesting and challenging. The first renewal effort, undertaken way before I got there, created a strip shopping center on the south side of the highway, Erie Boulevard, which ran through the downtown. By 1972, that center was not fully developed and in decline. The second phase of renewal was taking place on the north side of the Boulevard. The project was still in the property acquisition and demolishment stage when I started my job.

The premise upon which the second phase was originally planned was based on the declaration of most retail establishments located within the project area to stay and develop new facilities. This never worked out due to the complexities of the program and project already explained. In addition to the time factor, it was difficult to checkerboard a lot of businesses at once to allow for new infrastructure construction and the demolition of old buildings while enabling existing businesses to operate. So, as the project progressed, the focus on local redevelopment contracted.

The mayor, his staff, consultants and the full Urban Renewal Agency realized that it would be necessary to refocus and to try to attract new retail uses into the area, particularly large magnets such as a department store. One of the uses that were to be lost because of the difficulties of the project was the department store Goldberg's. It had always been intended that the business would rebuild within the project but that expectation failed.

The mayor wisely saw that the city would need help in navigating the marketing of sites to outside commercial interest. There was just no internal expertise of this nature. Largely through their local rep, we learned that the New York State Urban Development Corporation, UDC, was looking to expand its involvement in retail type projects. In short, UDC was created by New York State as a nonprofit development organization to spearhead housing and other forms of development throughout New York. It was headed by one of the country's premier local development experts, Ed Logue, who had headed Boston's very successful inner city redevelopment efforts. In Utica we had worked with UDC. It constructed the downtown Kennedy Apartment complex near City Hall. Logue had arrived by helicopter, landing right on the site to cut the construction ribbon and dig the first shovel. He sure had flair about him.

A team of us headed to Manhattan to see if UDC could help us with the project. We met with Peter Kory who had recently been named as the head of UDC's new commercial division. Kory was recruited from Cincinnati where he was that city's development director. He already had a great national reputation. His main claim to fame was the Cincinnati skywalks that linked retail and office centers in the downtown. This development technique is most known from Minneapolis, thanks to the Mary Tyler Moore show. Peter immediately liked us and we him. Shortly thereafter the Rome Urban Renewal Agency gave exclusive project development rights to UDC.

When Peter first looked at the downtown, he identified what he deemed to be its major impediment and one that would restrict the site's marketing potential. He concluded that a "split" downtown could not work. He felt that the existence of the strip center with surface parking, separated by a major highway would mean that shoppers would be forced to get into and out of their cars twice to shop in both areas. I was stunned at how obvious this was as he explained it and why we hadn't realized it sooner. Most retail developers would require a one stop, one parking shopping trip. This was particularly true of department store chains and their developers.

Kory's creative and exciting solution was to convince the new owner of the strip center to build new retail space in a straight line from the existing center to the tip of the highway and to physically link that space with an enclosed bridge that would cross over the highway and link with a shopping magnet on the other side. Shops could be located on the bridge itself. Rome, New York would have its own Ponte Verde. We labeled it the Living Bridge. Covered walkways would be added on the north side to offer shoppers weather protection wherever they shopped in the district. Obviously, the Rome "Living Bridge" was a variation of the Cincinnati sky walks.

Problems were identified. The basic one was to accept the premise that the average shopper would make the walk throughout the downtown. Peter strongly believed that the shopper would make the walk without thinking about it if attracted by enough retail outlets to offer interest and attention. The answer was stores and offices filling the spaces. The second need was to convince the strip center owner to bring retail attractions to meet the bridge. This meant that the center had to be expanded in that direction.

The city gave Kory and UDC the green light to put the plan together. It is conveniently forgotten that none of the renewal planning and implementation in Rome was done in private or as a secret. All plans and efforts required political and public review. This included City Council hearings and votes.

The new owner of the strip center was a developer named Jay Bonomo. Jay was from Connecticut and had several upstate commercial properties, including one on Bleecker Street in Utica. Jay was a nice guy and a successful but small developer. I knew him a little from my Utica days and got to know him very well in Rome. He and Kory also hit it off. Recognizing the logic of the plan and securing the all important carrot of UDC money to provide attractive financing, Bonomo came on board.

The next step was to convince the City Council to approve the Living Bridge. This was also accomplished but not without controversy and some hard convincing. UDC money in the form of a big grant that covered most of that cost was the convincer. The Council approved it up after some tense debate.

Thus two significant changes took place in the downtown development saga. They were the introduction of UDC with full development authority and the redesign of the project, resulting in physically linking the entire downtown. That change led to the change in the project's timing necessary to fit the new plan in a coordinated realistic fashion. Before I get into those, another key player should be introduced.

Charles Hilgenhurst headed the architectural firm that UDC and Rome used in the project's redesign. Charley was based in Boston, worked for Logue there and played a lead role in the design of Boston's wonderful City Hall/Government Center complex. Hilgenhurst's wife was a Roman and her parents still lived there. He was very familiar with the city as a frequent visitor. He and his firm designed the bridge, the new covered walkways and a new City Hall building that was to be located within the project. The Hilgenhurst approach had a distinct Boston flavor which I viewed as being very attractive. I think the Rome City Hall that was ultimately built is the nicest looking, modern City Hall in all of upstate New York. Many, including, future mayors did not share or appreciate the excellence Hilgenhurst gave them. In my opinion, their lack of good taste was telling.

Charley was to suddenly pass away as a relatively young man a few years after we both were finished with our work in Rome. I always felt it sad that his work was not more understood or appreciated in that city.

A decision that Bill Valentine himself made may have had an adverse effect on the ultimate success of the Living Bridge and of the entire renewal area. As I stated before, the entire premise of the bridge was to have it anchored by magnets to attract people to each side of Erie Boulevard. Bonomo upheld his end. On the other side, Marine Midland Bank agreed to construct a new bank on the west side. A large empty redevelopment parcel on the east side had to be developed to complete the full bridge concept and build magnet shopping attraction on that side.

Neither UDC nor we had been successful finding an anchor for that space. Bonomo came to us with the proposal that he would develop that space if the proposed City Hall would become part of it. His plan was to secure a long term city lease that would give him some financial security to develop the rest of a large retail structure. In other words City Hall would become a small part of a large retail center. The city lease would provide security that would allow Bonomo to finance the entire development. It would also bring City Hall workers and visitors directly to the living bridge. Jay presented this offer to me and our advisors. We liked it because it completed the entire effort to tie in both sections of the downtown with shopping and public gathering anchors. We decided to present it to the mayor. After serious consideration the mayor rejected Bonomo's plan. Valentine felt that the people's City Hall had to not only be owned by the people, but had to stand alone for proper recognition and respect. The mayor would not break away from the classic and historic in favor of the bold and different. He also expressed doubt of his ability to sell the idea to the city council and people of Rome. Today, that large piece of land still stands empty.

The Tale of Two Department Stores

One of the central, if not the central questions, that confronted most cities in the 1970s was whether or not major department stores could be kept or attracted into downtowns. Utica's downtown had lost Woolworths, Neisners, Kreskis and finally the Boston Store, all department stores. Major retail activities had and continued to shift to the suburbs. The New Hartford Shopping Center was followed by the Sangertown Mall ending any chance of downtown Utica remaining a retail center. Its downtown of past decades was forever dead. In Rome, many concluded that its ambitious downtown renewal project could not succeed. Although the timing of the Rome project flew in the face of retail development trends and evolution, Rome did have one ace in the hole. Rome had no suburbs. The existence of inner and outer districts, and a huge land area roughly the size of Los Angeles, gave Rome the ability to control development over this large land area through zoning laws and regulations. The city could thus direct development in ways most cities could not.

As Director of Planning between 1972 and 1977, and then as Director of Development from 1977 to the fall of 1979, one of the most important parts of my job was to do all I could do to help develop the downtown project in accordance with its renewal plan. Again, it must be repeated that the plan was the community's plan and was formally adopted as such. The federal, state and city governments had invested tens of millions of dollars in it. We had an obligation to do all we could to help it succeed.

As a result, municipal policy was to market the downtown to a major department store and to guard against development outside of the downtown area that could hurt that goal. All the demographic data we had indicated that the Rome market could only support a limited amount of retail space. So our effort to sell a downtown Rome location to a name department store was of great priority. We zeroed in on one.

JC Penney was targeted. Why that chain? I think there was a history of the store in Rome in the old days. Or that the third wife of founder James Cash Penney had a connection to Rome. The Rome Sentinel was also pushing it. Maybe Jay Bonomo got a lead. I do not recall all of the details. But we, meaning the whole Rome community, got behind an effort to convince the chain to bring a store to downtown Rome. Everyone got involved; the *Rome Daily Sentinel* carried out a public write-in campaign designed to show support. The impressive results were sent to JC Penney. Our efforts paid off when we were invited to New York City to meet with Penney officials. I'm hazy on the details of where we were when we got the call that JC Penney was coming to Rome but I'll not forget the sense of accomplishment we felt at that moment. The store continues to prosper in downtown Rome today.

Penney made the decision to lease the biggest building in Jay Bonomo's center, Rome's first urban renewal project area. Attracting that anchor was a highly positive sign but still left the task of attracting one on the north side, the Superblock. There were two vacant land site areas large enough to accommodate a department store. As we struggled to intensify our efforts there, Kmart came to town.

Kmart came to town in the person of Chicago based developer, Jack Jacobs. Jacobs was either the biggest or second biggest Kmart developer in the U.S. Kmart didn't develop their own stores but used private developers. Jack was a rich, well dressed, smart, smooth talking big city real estate developer. He was charming and direct. His dynamic personality made him appear much larger than his small physical frame. He was a short guy who loomed large.

A meeting was arranged for Jack to meet with the mayor and his development staff. At the meeting, which was both cordial and interesting, Jacobs explained that he wanted to develop a Kmart anchored shopping center on a site in West Rome, several miles from the downtown, along Erie Boulevard. We briefed him on the downtown project and asked him to consider doing his project there. He agreed to take a serious look at the possibility. He professed being open minded to the possibility of a downtown location.

Others and I gave him site tours and plenty of data. We also tried to entice him with a giveaway deal on either of two parcels in the project big enough to host a Kmart. One was the parcel next to the Living Bridge; the same one Bonomo had offered to develop with the new City Hall. Most of us sensed that the whole, "I'll take a look," commitment Jacobs waltzed through was simply a dog and pony show designed to result in his saying, "I tried," in turn for our support for his west Rome site. Why was it an obvious ploy? Developers like him did not make their money off of the Kmart's of the world; they made it through the leasing of space to other users in the center. Kmart was an anchor that paid cheap rent. Other, smaller retailers who wanted to locate in a Kmart center paid top dollar. That's where Jack made his profit. The downtown sites could only accommodate a Kmart. They were not big enough for him to develop the other stores. He could not make enough money downtown. And, I doubt he ever even discussed the possibility with Kmart. In other words, Jacobs was a shopping center developer, not strictly a Kmart developer.

Jacobs needed, or at least wanted, our support because he required a zoning variance to develop the west Rome site. I decided, with the mayor's support, to go to zoning war with Jack and Kmart, to deny them that location. The battle was waged for about a full year. We, put him through approval process hell. I fought it at every board level. The specifics are not all that important but an overview is. We suffered severe public criticism to an extent not before experienced. The consumer was angry. Very simply, the people wanted a Kmart and did not care where. The idea I held that we were obligated to fight against a development that could hurt the downtown project did not take public hold. And, forces like Carl Eilenberg, a popular local talk radio personality, were fanning the flames of public outcry. I also honestly felt that if we beat Jack in west Rome, we could force the Kmart development into the downtown. As I look back on that argument, it was a stupid Russian roulette ploy that was never going to work for reasons already discussed, most importantly, money, i.e. Jack's profit.

But the main reason I write of this episode of Rome's history is Bill Valentine. Deep down, the mayor also wanted a Kmart in Rome, period. He would also remind me all the time that he was even getting pressure at home because his beloved Hazel wanted Kmart! When he went on the street, most of what he heard was the pro Kmart opinion.

All he had to do to end the controversy was to tell me to call off the dogs. He did not. For as much as he wanted Kmart and as much as he wanted to end the controversy, he steadfastly stood behind the logic of defending the downtown effort and his staff. He did not cave.

Jacobs eventually got his west Rome development approval. He had to secure a very special City Council override of zoning and planning boards to get it, but he got it. During the months of fighting, which cost him time and money, Jack and I established a pretty friendly relationship. I liked him a lot as a person. He fought hard but was always a gentleman. I sensed that he liked me as well. As we walked out of the Common Council chambers the night he finally got the approval he needed he looked at me and said, "Rodger, you won." I said, "Jack, how did I win? You got your vote." He said, "because I know that when I get it built, you'll probably blow the f***in' thing up!" We laughed and shook hands.

Rome did get its Kmart in west Rome in later years. But, Jack did not build it. It got built after he, I and Bill Valentine were gone. The delays Jacobs experienced ran him and Kmart into a down period in which new projects were halted. By the time they started to build again, a different developer was involved. It exists today. In hindsight, I regret that Jack didn't build it and view my judgment and conduct as wrong. Experience has taught me that government and its bureaucrats cannot and should not shoe horn private business into decisions and locations that do not fit private enterprise business models. I, at the time knew little about business and had no right to try to force a square peg into a round hole.

Credit or Blame?

What happened in and to Rome's downtown has been the subject of controversy for decades. It has been a controversy of blindness and faulty revisionism. Before Urban Renewal, downtown Rome was in rapidly growing decline. The flight of shoppers to New Hartford and the Syracuse area was growing. The good old days were not very good. Under the leadership of Bill Valentine, Rome developed a respectable, prosperous, busy shopping center, complete with a JC Penney. By the end of Valentine's reign, one side of the downtown core was transformed into a very attractive area with a pedestrian mall. The other side featured an attractive covered walkway, brick sidewalks, a stunning new fountain and modern parking garages. New banks and new stores were constructed. The unique concept of the Living Bridge was developed. A reconstructed Fort Stanwix adjacent to the downtown was built and opened for tourists. These were all Valentine led accomplishments.

The failure was that a major shopping anchor like a JC Penney was not attracted to what was called the Superblock side of Erie Boulevard. The sites that were vacant the day Bill Valentine left office are vacant today, decades later. Why? There are two questions which no one can fully answer. If Valentine remained in office would the development have been successfully completed? Did it not get completed because those who followed Valentine in office were not up to task? The terms of Valentine's immediate successor, Carl Eilenberg, failed to add anything except a small subsidized elderly housing project to the downtown. Based on my development experience, I find it hard to believe that plans and adjustments could not have been made to develop the remaining vacant parcels with commercial value to the city and the downtown.

Instead of pulling out all stops to making something work, Eilenberg and the mayor who followed him, Joe Griffo allowed the area to stagnate. Griffo even took a wrecking ball and tore down the Living Bridge and the pedestrian mall. It is so easy to tear down; so much harder to build. Today, streets are back in and cars can drive and park in front of stores. But, guess what? No new development has taken place. Those who succeeded Valentine bear some of the responsibility along with changing demographics and market conditions.

The striking thing about Rome's experience was that even if it did not achieve its full plan, it still fared better than most. In Utica, for example, downtown renewal produced nothing but a public housing project and a hotel. In Rome the new downtown is better than the old. It fell short of the plan but did accomplish some unique change. Sadly, this change was not embraced by the community in ways that may have helped realize a more robust transformation.

What the planners and the city fathers did not recognize was that you can't impose the taste and standards of one area onto another.

In Rome's case, Kory, Hilgenhurst and we who worked with them tried to make Rome into a bricked, mini Boston with a Cincinnati type covered walk way. We brought an excellent level of aesthetics to the project but neglected the other redevelopment realities like weather, population demographics and expectations and the trends of small area developers to prefer suburban locations.

Ultimately, the city fathers, including Mayor Valentine, accepted a premise and process that ran counter to what their city could handle and fully digest. The primary architects of that premise, Kory and Hilgenhurst had far different futures. Kory went on to continue a celebrated urban development career and to this day is noted as a top notch national, urban land use expert. Hilgenhurst tragically had a stroke and passed way at a too young age.

I have frequently thought back to my days in Rome working with them and am still amazed that tiny Rome attracted their talent and expertise. Perhaps it was their hubris and our being taken with it that caused us to take an unrealistic shot at major center city transformation. I have asked myself the basic question every time I journey into Rome. Did leadership fail both during and after the Valentine administration or was the project unrealistic from the outset? I have concluded that it was a combination of both.

The Final Two Years

One might think that being named the Director of Community Development in 1977 would bring new activities and challenges to me. It did not. It was becoming increasingly clear that the downtown project was stalling. We did involve another private development group, Pioneer-Pyramid out of Syracuse to assist us in recruiting retail uses into the project but that was not meeting quick success. More seriously, with the election of a couple of new members, the City Council was turning political and argumentative. I started to publicly clash with them.

My conduct during that period was the low point in my professional career. I had no right whatsoever to take on elected representatives with the disrespect I displayed. In looking back at newspaper articles during that period, I'm amazed that Mayor Valentine didn't fire or censure me. The closest he came was to make a public statement that the quibbling stop on all fronts and that everyone role up their sleeves and get back to work for the good of the city. In all honesty, I think that many of us within the administration were burned out, including the mayor.

In the spring of 1979, Bill Valentine announced that he would not seek reelection in the fall. His political career after serving 16 years as mayor was over. The reason behind his decision was as much driven by his health than anything else. I, and others close to him, had been noticing that he wasn't himself for quite awhile. His memory had been noticeably slipping. By the time he decided not to run, I recall situations in which he discussed the same issue at least twice the same day. It was very upsetting to see his health failing. I can only imagine how hard it must have been for him.

I had decided to leave city government before the mayor's announcement and had been quietly looking at job alternatives. In particular, I was interested in opportunities with the state Urban Development Corporation. Although affiliated with the state, UDC was a private development corporation. It was one step away from government. When it soon became apparent that Carl Eilenberg, the local radio station owner and talk show host was to be the new Republican candidate for mayor, my resolve to leave got even stronger. I just could not imagine working with him under any circumstance.

As things heated up with UDC, one day in August I received a call from a local banker named Bob McGinty, asking if I would like to meet with him and another to discuss the job of heading the Oneida County Industrial Development Corporation. OCIDC was a non-profit development corporation run by the local business community. Bob was its chairman. I jumped at the opportunity. OCIDC was a mini-UDC but geographically limited to Oneida County. So, my ambition to start moving away from government could be realized while remaining in the area. After a series of interviews and discussions, I was offered and accepted the job of Executive Vice President of the organization. I left my Rome position in September of 1979.

Bill Valentine

I am not a Rome historian and cannot judge or comment on mayors that held office before Valentine. And, I was not on the inside working with mayors that succeeded him. But the historical record is clear; Bill Valentine was a leader far above most. Let's look at a summary of just some of his accomplishments.

He held the cost of government down, meaning taxes, as much as any mayor in any city or the state, if not the country. This was accomplished while providing a top notch level of city services. He did this in three fundamental ways. One, he hired and gave the proper level of power in financial matters to Dick Fahy, City Treasurer. Dick is perhaps the best example of several that demonstrates that Bill Valentine was not afraid of what I call hiring up. He was self assured enough to hire people who were smarter than he. Valentine's wisdom allowed him to be the decision maker while he allowed smart people to present him the choices. He did not have the inflated ego of many politicians that prohibited him from giving necessary free reign to the staff he hired.

This may sound trite to many readers but believe me it is not. In my experience, most politicians think much too highly of themselves to be effective leaders. Mayor Valentine had just the right combination of humility and strength. His personal characteristics were very similar to those of Dick Assaro. Both were extremely friendly and charming men in their own way. Both were not afraid to hire people who were smarter than they. Both were motivated by doing well for their communities. Both engendered great loyalty from those who worked for them.

The significant and important difference between the two leaders was in strength. Valentine could say a resounding firm no to anyone. He was clearly the boss, the decision maker. And he was not afraid to take public heat. Dick Assaro had a hard time saying no and sought a kind of universal approval from others. As a result, Dick could be more easily manipulated by others and events. Looking back on things, I wonder about several elements of the two mayors that might explain the difference.

Valentine's background was in sports, both as a top notch rough and tumble basketball player and a long time referee. He grew up and had years of having to make the right calls. I played in high school when he refereed. And, let me tell you, no player messed with Bill Valentine. Dick Assaro did not have an athletic background. Valentine worked in a mill. Dick was an undertaker. A mill is a rough place. As an undertaker, one always has to please a grieving family and the primary client doesn't talk back. Valentine was a huge, imposing man. You could not call him good looking but his stature made him so. Dick was short, and a sweet gentle man. He had a charm and warmth about him that was impossible not to embrace. He also had an all too human weakness of money and gambling. Valentine's big treat was to eat at a Red Lobster. He was a salt of the earth man with simple tastes.

As I play around with comparisons of the two mayors, I also wonder what the term length difference could have meant. A four year term allows for one to nurture more self confidence. A two year term rushes into yet another election. Over the years, I wonder how Dick Assaro would have evolved as a leader with more time. Valentine had that time.

As mayor, Bill Valentine did lead under a period of great stability and some growth while other upstate cities started their decline. His tax policies and record of providing excellent city services were major reasons why Rome's population and neighborhoods thrived. There was no slum in Rome. The reversal of the Air Force's decision to move RADC provided the continuation of a most important economic and social feature of the city and the area. Although Valentine was but one player in the effort, he brought it together and led its cooperative framework.

Bill's efforts to create and complete a downtown revitalization effort have been discussed in detail. But, a key point not discussed was the effort's boldness. Valentine did not attack the problem half heartedly. He tackled an immense effort in a relatively small town. This took both political courage and strength. He dared to tackle a problem in ways that most mayors would have avoided. But, his real strength was more citywide.

Bill Valentine's philosophy was based on neighborhood preservation. He understood and appreciated city life. Resources were dedicated to Rome's neighborhoods, particularly in parks and street paving. There was no fluff in his budgets. Amazingly, he served 16 years without an executive assistant and just one secretary. Take a look at mayors today. They have assistants, publicity aides, two or more secretaries and all kinds of people and programs that do nothing for the real problems and priorities.

What I recall most about Bill Valentine was his basic honesty. He was honest with you and expected you to be honest with him. There was no malarkey or baloney about him. He trusted and enjoyed people and was extremely loyal to those around him. He got back that loyalty in return.

Everywhere we seemed to go, whether it is the streets of Boston, New York City, Washington D.C. or Utica, someone would yell out, "Hey Bill," or, "Bill, how are you?" He was a well known, deeply liked and respected guy. He died at age 77. When I last saw the mayor, he was at a nursing home. He looked straight at me and had no idea who I was. I wish I had never gone.

Rome should do more for and in the memory of one terrific person and mayor.

The Two Cities

The existence of two central cities located a scant 20 miles from each other in one county has been both a curse and a blessing. History shows it to be more of a former than the latter. Given that this book focuses primarily on the political, there is one aspect of how politics was practiced in the two cities that is both interesting and telling. A few personal tales illustrate these differences.

As I served the final years of my stint in Utica as the mayor's executive assistant, my public profile grew. With that, it was assumed that I held sway. After all, sitting next to the throne, any throne, is a position of at least influence, if not great power. In most places, I would assume it makes one a political target.

In the first section of this book, the destruction of Fred Nassar as a political goal was described. I experienced similar attempts on a smaller, but nevertheless disturbing scale. Early at my desk one morning, I was reviewing the schedule of the day while the mayor sat in his office doing the same. Our standard practice was for each to arrive about an hour before the 9 AM workday started, review matters separately and then meet to discuss them once our thoughts were formulated. That morning, I looked up and saw a man sitting out in the lobby staring intently at me. He did not look happy. I recognized him as a Carbone. He was a family member of one of the largest automobile dealerships in the area. Dick Assaro walked out of his office and asked me to join him and Carbone in the mayor's office. When we sat, Dick explained that Carbone called him earlier that morning and said that someone saying he was Rodger Potocki called and tried to extract the pledge of a big political contribution. He was very upset. I, who had never asked anyone, let alone him for a nickel, was put in the position to defend something either unethical or illegal that someone had tried to pin on me with an early morning fake call to someone I had never even met, let alone called. Was he sitting there trying to ascertain the truth in the matter by the sound of my voice? Did he honestly believe that making a call like that was something I would do outside and before my normal 8 AM morning routine?

Another time, my wife received an afternoon call telling her that I just checked into a motel with another woman. I had taken the afternoon off. What the caller did not know was that I had taken the time on a family matter and that I was at home, with my wife when the call was made! But, here was another attempt to defile and hurt someone, me and my family, in a serious personal way.

These are, or at least were, examples of politics in Utica. My father used to tell the story of William Rogers, who practiced law for a period in Utica. He went on to be Richard Nixon's first Secretary of State. My father quoted Rogers as saying, "Utica was the roughest town I ever worked in." He was right.

In Rome, politics was not personal. By and large, political fights were rare and respectable. I often speculated that analyzing the two communities on a sociological basis would have made for an interesting study. What was in the character of Utica residents that made them rougher than most? Did this roughness spill over into areas beyond politics? Did the Valentine influence and length of his service have a taming effect on the city in general? Did the concentration of criminal elements in the larger Utica play the central role in defining the city? Having lived and served in both cities, I certainly know that their residents sure view themselves as being different. What is at the heart of this perception: size, ethnic difference, level of wealth, lack of suburbs in Rome? Two cities so close, so dominated by Italian American populations and possessing other similarities should not be all that different. But they are.

We know that Rome has no history of major crime or boss politics. Perhaps it was too small to attract either. I don't know enough about the ethnic differences among the Italian settlers of both cities. This topic may make for an interesting book by someone else. A study of the commercial history of both cities may enlighten. I can make one observation I think critical.

Rome was home to the Griffiss Air Force Base. The base, in turn, as being military brought many people from all over the country into Rome. Some were high level officers, some pilots, some intelligence experts. Some stayed for short stints, some long. Most brought families. These families got involved in the community on all levels; in churches, schools, social groups and all forms of community interaction. Over the years many retired and settled in Rome.

This coming, going and staying of new blood with experience from all over the nation and in some cases international opened Rome to new ideas, influences and experiences. Utica, through the history that I've experienced has been an insulated city, one with not much outside penetration. As such, it stayed old and unchanging in most important ways.

Only until recently, with the influx of "new" immigrants has the outside come into Utica since going way back to the early 1900's. This is now bringing change. There are fascinating questions of the impact of this change. Again, that is not a topic for this book. But, it already has led to a different Utica. And, it could be argued that Rome is now the more insular, for better or for worse.

Both cities face uncertain futures. They have both hemorrhaged population. Today, they are about half the size they were forty years ago. The loss of the air base severely hurt Rome in several ways. Costs associated with government continue to escalate forcing higher taxes. This, in turn, leads to more population loss. Neither city has carved out new, modern identities or growth strategies. As of this writing the Rome is led by Jim Brown, a Mayor whose career was in the private sector. He has restored more fiscal responsibility to the city government. More will be said of Utica in a future chapter. Its leadership problems and political rancor continue to plague the city. Its current social and economic problems are severe, to say the least. Both cities are shadows of their past histories. Both have experienced a decline hard to fathom just a relatively short time ago.

I recently had a conversation with a smart man who made the observation that Rome has a history of fighting change that is encouraged and promoted by those who control the status quo. I don't totally buy into that conclusion but it is a reoccurring theme that appears throughout this book. More than most, both cities and to a large extent, the entire area, has in many ways resisted and sometimes fought change. The roots of this characteristic are found in its ethnic, social, economic and political character. This inability to grasp the need for basic change in its institutions and hostility to new ideas was found in both cities by this author at a relatively young age. The nature of its people may have more to do with the failure to foster positive and creative change, not some nefarious plot by the establishment.

Chapter Three

County Executives & Business Development—
1979-1994

The Oneida County Industrial Development Corporation was a non-profit business development group governed by the Oneida County business community. It received its funding from several sources. The majority came from annual private business contributions and fees resulting from development projects including land sales. The government of Oneida County contributed relatively small amounts on an annual basis. OCIDC owned the Oneida County Airport Industrial Park located in Oriskany, served as the focal point and coordinating body for most new industrial development projects anywhere in the County, and issued financing for projects through its own loan fund. It also issued development project bonds through its sister agency, the Oneida County Industrial Development Agency. It was a multipurpose, private development corporation charged with assisting job creation and business growth in Oneida County.

When I became its Executive Vice President in October 1979, the organization was in trouble. It was running out of support and money, had not had any major projects in a few years, and was not viewed as effective by the County of Oneida and both cities. My task was to rebuild the organization. Although the 15 years I spent doing that offers a description of a very successful and rewarding experience on many levels, such is not the purpose of this chapter or book. Since part of that purpose is to offer insight into political leadership and its effectiveness the OCIDC years will be described in a limited fashion by relating details of particular projects and how they were impacted by elected officials and politics. This will provide an interesting and telling look at people and events that shaped and, in some ways, continue to shape the Utica-Rome area.

Metropolitan Life—Sherry Boehlert

Metropolitan Life had opened a small back office operation in Utica in 1969. The OCIDC assisted Met in that project. That started a trusted, productive relationship between the companies. In particular, a good rapport had developed between an OCIDC staffer, Jim Kellmurray, and a New York City based Met Vice President, Bob Muller. Bob was the executive who among other things oversaw the operations here.

When I assumed my position, Kellmurray had been holding down the OCIDC fort during the protracted absence of an Executive VP. I became Kellmurray's supervisor. Because of his relationships and experience with Met Life, Jim remained our key contact with them. In late 1979, Jim informed me that the company was considering a major back office expansion out of New York City and that our area was considered a prime location. The company loved the work force it had come to know in Utica for reasons of both cost and productivity. The labor factor had put us in the running for the expansion.

I was quickly brought up to speed on Met Life and started meeting with their key players, both in person and on the phone. Their point man continued to be Mueller. Bob was an extremely smart, down to earth, old school kind of guy and we quickly hit it off. He confirmed Met's plan to expand and since they were in a small location in Utica, laid out the details of the type of spot they would need for a much larger operation. He wanted his team to see all existing building and new construction sites here that could meet their specs. Most critically, he swore us to secrecy.

No company wants to undergo the site selection process in public for a myriad of reasons. They include the effect on price, time, impact on existing work force, and the absolute disdain for being embroiled in public disputes among competing locales and political entities. Most companies, particularly the big ones, simply will not touch areas that do not pledge to honor the rule of confidentiality.

We started our work and prepared a comprehensive package of information on many different sites in the county. Muller and his team were up frequently to look at and discuss possibilities. We even took them on a helicopter ride to see locations from above. It was OCIDC's policy, that the goal was to land the deal and that the best way to do that was to expose the client to all available locations in our county. We did not care where they went as long as they came to Oneida County. In this case, we were showing them sites in Utica, Rome and at our Airport Park. Under conditions of confidentiality, we did inform key locals, including some political office holders, of the project. That included Oneida County's new County Executive Sherwood Boehlert. He was an ex-congressional aide to Al Pirnie and, as mentioned in the previous section, tried to succeed Pirnie. When Don Mitchell took the seat he kept Sherry on staff. Boehlert came back to the area to run for county executive in 1979. No one who knew anything about him doubted that he viewed that job as a stepping stone to someday filling the congressional seat.

I had known Boehlert for a long time. He was a high school acquaintance of my older sister and as a Pirnie aide, was known for years by all involved in local government and politics. I liked him and was strongly in his corner during the county race. I thought he would be an effective county leader and looked forward to working with him, as did most of my board members.

At the time of the Met inquiry, an existing empty office building of top of the line quality was available at our park. It was the former headquarters of a huge local success story, Mohawk Data Sciences. MDS was eventually bought out by a New Jersey based company, which moved the work done here to New Jersey, thus vacating the building. The building was impressive and fit Met's space requirements. It also was one of the best real estate deals in the country. The price being sought was well below the value of the building in relation to its construction cost. It was a Cadillac building at a Ford price. The Met team loved it. The only complication was that another company was interested in it. Once it became clear that Met Life was the preferred buyer, the deal was set. We were to help structure the financing package.

I was informed in late May of 1980 that the deal was done. Met was going to buy the building and bring nearly 500 jobs to the area. We were told not to make the decision public until the company gave the green light. I immediately informed the County Executive, and strongly informed him that Met was insisting on complete secrecy until they were ready to make an announcement.

It is also important to note that I made it clear to Boehlert that he would be in the forefront of publicity on the project at announce-ment time. Both OCIDC and Met Life, understood politics and politicians. We all knew that politicians love to take credit for jobs. Throughout my career at OCIDC, which was to last 15 years, I made sure the elected officials got their public relations due. It was a smart way to build our organization's strength and it was smart for me personally. In this case, we were prepared to give Boehlert part of center stage as soon as the company would give the go ahead for a public announcement. Met was not yet ready to do so. The company was sensitive to informing its employees who would be transferring into the area, as well as those who would be relocated from Utica to Oriskany. Since they were relocating their small Utica operation to the airport park, they also wanted to inform the Utica mayor of their decision.

When Sheardown saw that building, his eyes lit up. I found out why later, when on my first trip to see his plant in Canada, I noticed it was almost the exact replica of the Corl building. We then finished our tour of the Rome site which did not interest him.

Grawbowski had been with us all day but had an early evening engagement to attend. Sheardown and I sat down at a bar in Utica to have a beer and to discuss the day. He indicated that he really liked the Corl building but was a, "man of his word", meaning he was committed to Batavia. In fact, he was meeting that night with their industrial development board on his way back to Toronto. I was curious about the deal he was getting there. The Batavia folks had packaged the deal in a pretty standard fashion, with low interest money and some tax breaks. I expressed surprise when he didn't mention any job training grants. I outlined a package of training grants his company would be eligible for to offset new hire costs. When I finished, he asked me if he could get the same deal in Batavia. Although I hated to admit it, I told him yes, because the funds were from the state. Therefore, Batavia would be eligible to tap them just as we could. He immediately turned red. He told me that if that were true and he found out that the Batavia people were, holding out on him, all bets were off on his commitment there and that he would seriously look at Oneida County. He went on to tell me that he would ask them that night and call me early the next morning to let me know what happened. The next morning he called and said that I was right. They had not offered the training grants and he did want to seriously consider the Corl Building. That started the effort to put the purchase deal together which involved our organization and the involved local banks.

He wound up buying and occupying the building. The first day I walked in as the first 30 or so new Bus Industries of America employees were at work, I was emotionally moved. The site of people working to feed families in a building that had been totally vacant really got to me. Thanks to Carmen Arcuri, and my Batavia counterpart, we landed the project. The company is still there, expanded and now named, Daimler Bus of North America. Over 700 work there in manufacturing jobs. Don Sheardown had grown the company successfully here and in Canada until he was bought out. He passed away soon after retirement. He was a good man.

I think Sherry Boehlert was still Oneida County Executive at the time Bus first came in. And he wasn't informed of the project too early to risk premature publicity. I was not going to be burned twice. Soon after, Sherry realized his dream to become Congressman. He and Sheardown developed a close friendship and Sherry was very helpful to the company on the federal level. This ultimately contributed significantly to the growth of the company here.

Boehlert ran for the seat as the endorsed Republican candidate in the 1982 Congressional election after Mitchell retired unexpectedly. He won and went on to serve 12 terms! He also vacated his position as county executive early to give his successor a leg up on the job. This was to start what turned out to be a too common practice of appointing Oneida County Executives.

I thought Boehlert's rise was an amazing accomplishment for a guy who was not the best and brightest. Since my direct business dealings with Sherry were few after he was county exec, he won't appear much throughout the remainder of this book. So, I'll summarize my impressions of his leadership ability and record. It should be noted that I've had kind of a love-hate relationship with him over the years. Personally, I admire where he started and where ended in his career. In short, he achieved a great deal in his personal journey from extremely humble beginnings to a 12 term congressman. And, in many ways I found him to be a very nice guy and good family man.

In terms of his job performance, the loss of Griffiss Air Force Base, the constant shrinking of Rome Labs and the population loss of his district during his term have to lead to questioning his overall effectiveness. I had always felt that protecting Griffiss and growing the labs were the primary jobs of anyone holding that seat. He failed on both scores. My sense is that his rebel, RINO (Republican in Name Only) status in D.C. lost him the seat on the powerful Armed Services Committee, which certainly had to impact his effectiveness in military matters. He also failed to deal with the Oneida Indian land dispute issue early on at the federal level. This issue, which plagues and poisons the region to this date, could have been resolved early in the game with strong Boehlert leadership. He would not touch it. Finally, I find it strange that someone who spent every waking hour while in office extolling our area as the greatest anywhere would hustle off to the beaches of Delaware right after he no longer needed our votes. And to think, Rehoboth Beach doesn't even need his pension dollars!

Met Life II

Metropolitan Life Insurance has also had a long, successful history at its Oriskany location. It now employs over 1,000 people. There is an interesting slant to the company's second major expansion, which took place in 1993. In contemplating that expansion, Met had an alternate location somewhere in Florida in mind as a possibility. We were told that Oneida County was the front runner but that some in the company felt that it might make sense not to concentrate too many people at one location. As before, we were plugged in to what was going on with the understanding that the project would be confidential until otherwise notified.

At some point in the process, the Utica *Observer Dispatch* caught wind of it and the possibility that the Florida location was in the mix. A story had appeared in the Florida media. Well, the *OD* started to speculate whether we would lose an expansion and if so,

I would have to explain why. They were eager to predict loss and to point fingers as to why. I, and the county executive at the time, knew what the real scoop was but could not, and would not, discuss it publically. Met appreciated that. We landed the expansion and the *OD* had to eat crow.

At some point in the process, our development team went to a national insurance industry convention. The head of Met Life was in attendance with his wife. As was common practice at these business conventions, there was an area for business booths where companies and groups like ours would pitch their wares to the attendees. Most exhibitors gave gifts to entice people over to the booth. Our big gift prize was a beautiful tea set that Oneida Silver had donated to us. It was probably the nicest grand prize at that convention. The Met president's wife loved it. By some strange twist of luck, his business card was picked out of the jar! He was one happy guy. We had a very warm conversation with him and were told how much the company loved Oneida County. Of course, we rigged every drawing we ever had at every convention we attended. Did this little gesture help land that expansion? We'll never know but our gesture could not have hurt. This type of taking a little edge does not get publicity but has a way of paying off.

The Plumley Years—1982-1991

An old golfing buddy frequently uses the expression, "They aren't as dumb as they look," as a playful warning that city people ought to be wary of farmers. Jack Plumley is from the small, rural village of Camden, located in northwestern Oneida County. One from a city would call those from Camden, farmers. Jack neither looked, nor was, dumb. He was as street smart as one you'd ever meet. He had rugged outdoorsman written all over him. Even today he is a healthy looking, strong, elderly man you'd still be hesitant to cross. In 1982, he was appointed Oneida County Executive to succeed Sherry Boehlert.

Plumley was a successful businessman who had his hands deeply into Republican politics. He had several businesses in Camden, including a real estate company and a hardware store. He was a hunter and a fisherman of great talent and repute. Politically, he started as a young protégé of Harold Kirch who was mentioned earlier as the guy who pretty much ran the county as head of the Board of Legislators prior to the switch to a county executive form of government in the early 1960s. Jack took over Kirch's board seat and eventually also became board chairman. So, in many ways, he was a natural to succeed Boehlert. This started a pattern of Republicans designations of County Executives upon early exits of incumbents. That process was to be repeated three consecutive times after the Plumley precedent. It would turn out to be a negative pattern for the health of the area but a highly successful one for maintaining Republican Party control. The key reasons of advantage include the ability of incumbents to raise lots of money and the control of patronage jobs.

I had only known Plumley slightly when he became Oneida County Executive. What I did know of him, I liked a lot. Unlike Sherry Boehlert, there was no double talk from Plumley. He was direct and frank. As they say, he called 'em like he saw 'em. He also understood the implications of his being a businessman first, and a politician, second. His image as a tough, conservative was matched by his actions in governing. He played politics but did not need politics. That kind of self assurance sort of reminded me of Bill Valentine in certain ways. As it turned out, I don't think the working relationship we had could have been much better. I'm going to use a couple of examples that highlight the years we worked together. One describes an extremely successful effort; the other a failure for the area. However, overall the years in which

Jack Plumley was county executive and I was the head of OCIDC brought huge success to the economy of the Oneida County.

There are four basic reasons why that type of partnership was essential to our development world. First, the business atmosphere government creates, particularly in the form of tax policy, is extremely important to all aspects of business development. Plumley ran a tight fiscal ship. That is particularly important in the recruitment of companies concerned with cost and area stability. Second, in many ways, whether it is a public works component like a road, or a job training program, or in some cases, use of public land, government often plays a direct role in projects. In our case, it was the county and its subunits that were often needed to help aspects of, deal packaging. If the relationship was not smooth, cooperative, efficient and confidential, a project could never happen or could suffer. Third, our organization did receive part of its funding from the county. Although it was not the majority of our funding, its elimination would have caused problems. Finally, a prospect always wants to meet the political leadership of the community at some stage of the development process. Political atmosphere as indicated by political leadership is important to the measuring of a community. At the OCIDC, we always let the company we were courting or working with determine when elected leaders were to be met. When the time came, Plumley's style and business background made a great impression on our clients. He also understood that his role was defined by the company with whom we were working and not by political opportunism. He was content to remain in the background until the proper time. In that respect, he was very different than Boehlert who viewed all matters through his personal political prism.

Many years after Jack left office and I left the OCIDC, we would occasionally cross paths. We both marveled at the over 15,000 new jobs that were created in the years we worked together in close harmony. The then Norstar bank operations center; the huge

Met expansion; AFSA Data; Hartford Insurance; the bus company expansion; the Utica Business Park projects with Bendix and GE; the creation of the first private business loan program that created many new smaller companies and helped several key local expansions; and the Irving Trust/Bank of New York development were many of the larger ones. Several remain today as mainstays of the Oneida County economy. Each has a story and each certainly involved many others in addition to the county executive. But, I'm not too sure that many would have happened had it not been for the area's key player's ability to work effectively together. I'm going to use one example at length to describe how working together succeeded in a significant accomplishment. As good, coordinated, effective leadership can lead to success, poor leadership and rotten politics assure failure. Sadly, a major loss experienced in the same general period of the gain severely damaged the area. The two stories provide insight into the good and the bad. It is up to the reader to identify the ugly.

The Bank Job

In early 1988, I received a direct call from a business and real estate consultant out of the New York City area, indicating that he represented a client who was looking at locations for relocating a substantial number of financial, back office type jobs out of the city. As is always the case in any real inquiry of any size, the client was not named and a laundry list of information was requested ASAP. Just about all of the information requested at this stage was labor and site related. I immediately agreed to provide the information in the time frame specified. I also notified my board president, Dave Grow and county executive Jack Plumley of the call. Why? As a matter of practice, I notified Dave of everything we were working on. In Plumley's case, I wanted him to notify key county agencies such as Planning, that if I called and asked for information, they were to hustle and provide it. And, I trusted Jack and his people to maintain confidentiality whenever required. We had been using Mike Gapin and his excellent planning department as our county coordinating arm on many projects over the years, but would always notify their boss, Plumley, before calling Mike. My staff and I, with the help of Gapin and others, put the package together. The "others" have to be described to truly understand how things were handled in those days. They were Steve DiMeo, Utica's development director, Ron Conover, his Rome counterpart, and Ed Ratazzi of the Rome Industrial Development Corporation.

These people were a part of our on-going team approach to development. They were plugged in on every project we worked on if a project could affect Utica or Rome. They, in turn, were responsible for keeping their bosses informed as they saw fit. And, they always respected our lead in determining when. During this period, Lou LaPolla was the mayor of Utica; Carl Eilenberg, of Rome. Both respected and understood confidentiality and all operated in an atmosphere of trust. We had come a long way since the fist Met project.

How was this trust built? A good deal of the credit goes to Jack Plumley. The mayors knew, as I did, that Jack was a straight shooter and would not try in any way to undercut or harm the cities' job development efforts. They knew politics was not the end all be all for Jack. On the staff level, all knew that we, OCIDC, would include any and all city locations on the site lists we prepared for clients. A day rarely went by when I did not talk with Steve, Ron or Ed on the phone. They also understood that I didn't care where a project happened as long as it happened here and that making the client aware of all locations that fit maximized our chances of winning the project. They knew I would not mislead them in any way. The role of my board president during most of this period was important as well. Dave Grow was an attorney from Rome with whom I worked in the Valentine administration. We had a history of trust and friendship. He was also a jock and a regular guy. Dave had a sound relationship with Plumley going way back. Both had solid Republican Party credentials, lineage and, good names. The fact that they were from the western end of the county helped. Perhaps most important and, surprising, the cities with their years of distrust actually pulled together during this period. That cooperation is one of the reasons for the success experienced.

During the terms of Lou LaPolla in Utica and Carl Eilenberg of Rome, the historical distrust and back biting between the cities was nonexistent when it came to industrial development. This network of leadership was to play out in an extremely positive way as we started to deal with the NYC call and the project it represented.

Step one was to inform all of the call and let them know that we were including city sites in our package of information. As a group, we double checked the inventory we had, and discussed which particular sites worked and which did not.

Seven were submitted that fit the company's specs. They included four sites that could accommodate new construction and three existing buildings. Two new construction sites were in Rome, one in Utica and one located at our Oriskany airport business park. Our favorite existing building was the former Boston Store in Utica's downtown. This was our favorite site for several reasons. It held a special place in the heart of the city and in mine. The Boston Store was part of the city's rich history as the anchor to a thriving city center. When it emptied, a huge scar of better days was left behind. Filling it would be a huge booster to Utica. My mother worked in the Boston Store for 37 years! I had my hair cut in her shop when I was a young boy and bought my last pair of white bucks there at the store's closing sale. How I would love to tell my mom that we were filling the old store with new jobs.

The labor data was extensive and related to work force availability, cost and productivity. As in all cases, labor is the key to clinching a deal. If you don't have enough at the right price compared to other areas, you lose! I was to find out later that in this case, the labor factor was even more important than most. We submitted our package and waited.

Not that long after we submitted, I got the call from the front man that the client was sending a team to the area to meet with us and to start reviewing the information in greater detail. I don't recall how, but I learned that the client's team leader for that initial meeting was a guy who loved basketball. I hoped I could use my own basketball background to help establish a quick, positive vibe between us.

We hosted the meeting in a private room at a new restaurant that had been created out of an old firehouse in West Utica. It was a neat place with an urban flavor, one that we thought would impress the New Yorkers. The meeting was confidential and was only attended by the client's team, my staff and I. They were there and seated as we arrived. I walked up to their head guy who was seated at the head of the table. Before we even shook hands, I said, "I hear you like basketball. I'll tell you what. We'll play a game of one on one and if I win, your company comes here!" Or something to that effect. He stood up and I almost fainted. He was a huge Chinese American guy who was taller than I and a lot bigger in the muscle department. I realized instantly that he would kick my butt in a one on one game. We shook hands and laughed. His name was Dominic Chang and he worked for the Irving Trust Corporation, a large New York City based bank located in the Wall Street area of lower Manhattan.

We had a productive working lunch. There was an instant good rapport with the Irving guys and us. It's hard to put into words but sometimes you just quickly like people, and have a good feel. Such was the case with Dominic and his team. I could only hope they liked us as much. As I've indicated, I was always a believer in the idea that personal relationships count an awful lot in business. If two areas are close to what a prospect wants, a friendship can be the difference in the final choice. Anyway, that lunch started what was to become a very profound business and personal project for me. And, it became very important to Oneida County and all of central New York.

After that first meeting, we quickly learned that the project would involve over 400 jobs being initially relocated from New York City. These jobs carried out deposit service and international funds transfer operations, a key part of Irving's income stream. The bank would try to relocate key top managers but would hire most other employees from the local labor force. A key part of their plan hinged on the lower labor cost here, combined with higher productivity. They were also looking to locate in close proximity to a Federal Reserve Center, which we had at the Oneida County Airport.

The process started at that meeting and was quickly followed up with showing alternative sites to the Irving people as they continued their visits. That brought their key Irving executive into the picture. This top level manager was Jim Ganley a senior executive vice president for operations. Since Ganley and Chang were going to spend days actually looking at sites here, it was obvious that the matter would quickly become public. Some of the existing building sites were privately owned and we would have to inform the owners of the need to get into the buildings. We decided to do a controlled leak of the project and that we were in the running for it. We publically confirmed interest by an unidentified client. We also learned that Richmond, Virginia was our main competitor for the project.

As sites were toured, a very telling and half funny/half disheartening experience took place in Utica. The former Boston Store was designated by the Irving group early on as the only existing building that they would be interested in. As a result, that was the only building shown to Ganley when he came in for the tour. I'll not forget the day. As we looked at the building, Ganley liked it a lot. He actually liked the idea of an urban location thinking it would benefit their workers in several ways. It was relatively early in the morning in a near deserted downtown when we left the building. We walked out the front door and headed for our cars when from out of nowhere, a bum who was extremely dirty and obviously had a drinking problem went up to Ganley and started pestering him for money. The guy was persistent and we didn't want to create an ugly scene. But, I could have choked the guy! That, on the spot, ended whatever chance downtown Utica had to get the project. When Ganley got in the car he used an expletive to give Utica thumbs down. Imagine, here a bank was looking for a quiet, safer spot than big, bad New York City and their senior decision maker gets grabbed and sort of mugged right on Genesee Street!

The site Irving did love was located at the airport in our industrial park. It was right near the Fed, was served by the airport, had plenty of size and was almost directly adjacent to the Met Life Building. The Met Life connection was much more important than I realized at the time.

The bank was in a hurry to get moving. They had a strict timetable related to the relocation and Ganley and Chang were charged to make it happen. The rush was to be better understood by us later.

Thus a flurry of trips started many of Irving's key players coming here and of us going there. On either the first or second trip of Ganley, I was asked to arrange a dinner for him and Dominic Chang to meet the county executive. I learned from Dominic that Jim appreciated the finer things in life including, fine dining and good wine. So, I selected one of our area's most upscale restaurants, the Horned Dorset, for the dinner. It was also out of the way, in the rural southern part of the county and had private rooms for business talk and drinks. Two things were apparent at the dinner.

The bank guys really took to Jack Plumley and he to them. He regaled them with stories of his hunting and fishing escapades. They brought their big city tales. Jim also fell in love with the Horned Dorset. We learned that the bankers were avid golfers. We, in turn, described the many wonderful golf courses our area offered. All in all, the night could not have gone better. It was if we all had been friends for years.

As things turned out, every time Jim Ganley was to come to the area and that was often, he insisted on two things; that Jack join us for dinner and that we go to the Horned Dorset. It was to be a couple of years before I was able to get him to another restaurant. Plumley, being a man of simple, down home tastes, quickly got tired of the fanciest, most expensive restaurant in the area. Every time I called him to tell him the Irving guys were coming in and they wanted him to join in dinner, he'd say, "Dammit, Rodger, do we have to go to the Horned Dorset again?" Long fancy dinners with expensive wine, impeccable service and cigars were not for Jack. I don't think that could have been said for many politicians.

We, meaning myself and Dave Grow, journeyed to Irving's offices at 101 Barclay Street a couple of times early in the game as well. We met more people there, including their construction guys, to answer questions about how soon they could get into the ground if we were selected. They thought we were nuts when we said we could get them permitted in 30 days and would even give them early entry on the site. In other words, they could start before the legal, ownership transfer would take place. I'll never forget the first time we went to meet with them at their home base.

Dominic arranged for us to bunk at the bank's condo which was located kitty corner from 101 Barclay on Greenwich Street. We got in the night before the meeting and had dinner with several of the Irving people. Chang met us in front of the office early in the morning. He had to walk us through lobby security. As we got on the elevator, workers were streaming in. A whole bunch knew

Dominic and must have been part of the functions that were going to be relocated. In the elevator, they started to chant, "Richmond, Richmond, Richmond." Everyone except us laughed. It was pretty clear where those employees wanted to go. They had no idea who Dave and I were but we were sure sick to hear the chant. On the way home, I wondered aloud to Dave whether or not we had a chance to bag the deal. Deep down I doubted our area's chances to beat Richmond. I was wrong.

To make the proverbial long story short, by August 1988 it was announced that Irving Trust would build the new facility at the Oneida County Airport and initially employ 425 people. We did beat Richmond!

How we even got on the Irving list to begin and why we won the deal have significant meaning. I found out later directly from Jim Ganley that the head of Irving, was a golf buddy of the head of Met Life. During a golf match, hearing that the bank was looking for locations to move functions, the Met board chairman suggested that the Utica area be looked at since Met was so happy there. That's how we made the initial list. Golf even gave us more of an edge than we knew at the time. Our great relationship with Met paid off in spades. Perhaps the tea set gesture meant more than we ever thought it would.

It quickly became apparent that Ganley and Chang were not just avid golfers; they were degenerate golf junkies. Coming here, they could easily drive up in a few hours, do their business and get a round of golf in. I know, because early on I arranged the golf and joined them. Did the ease and availability of great golf courses help? Of course it did. If an area is not attractive to key decision makers in a personal way, an area may not even get the opportunity to satisfy the business concerns and criteria.

Were the close, fun relationships that quickly developed here important? I like to think that we hit it off in ways that were not matched by our counterparts in the Richmond area. All of these things fit into the success formula. But, we would not have gotten as far as we did if not for the basics to the bank's business concerns. The bottom line of profit trumps all else. That is what business is all about. And, the cost and productivity of the workers is the most basic of all.

With the help of the local State Labor Department, we compiled extensive labor data for Irving. That even includes responses to blind employment ads that were run. And, I'm sure they did network with companies like Met to check out performance and cost. The availability of labor is one thing; the dollars and cents labor translation is another. In that sense, a labor force made up of local people ultimately wins business development projects. Our job was to make sure the story got told in as complete and accurate terms as possible.

Second, you must have a site that works. We were able to package a large site of about 90 acres that would accommodate expansion and deliver it at in a more than timely manner. The fact that OCIDC owned the land cut price negotiation time and allowed for things like early entry. We did deliver the permitting in 30 days and in June of 1989, the doors opened and over 200 employees walked in. By then, the bank was not Irving Trust but the Bank of New York.

During the construction process, the takeover of Irving by the Bank of New York played out. The takeover was a hostile one and we then understood that one of the reasons for the rush to get the project underway was to help resist the takeover. Plus, the Irving guys did not know how the Bank of New York would view the move if they took over. We were scared to death that BONY, as it was then called, might pull the plug on the project. That did not happen, thank God. I suspect that labor also played a role in avoiding a change.

The project was being fast tracked; that included early hires that were shipped to New York for training and local hires that were being trained in an old mill building in Utica. My sense is that the types of employees that were being attracted and trained were solid proof that the relocation made financial and productivity sense to BONY once they took a look at what Irving had accomplished. Well, the project happened. At writing, 850 or so are employed in the Utica area and over 900 are in the Syracuse area. The company is now BNY Mellon, the Bank of New York having merged with Mellon Financial. The facilities here are true success stories for the bank and the community. Valuable new blood for the community was relocated from the City and hundreds of locals were hired.

The Irving Trust story is a great example of how a community can grow jobs. The foundation of the effort reflects the leadership qualities that were present and necessary to win a major development. It wasn't the largest, or the first, or last. But, it is one of the most informative. It is also the one of many projects I was involved in that turned out to change the course of my life. How those changes came about and what they meant will be discussed later.

In researching this book, I was reminded that the period in which the now BNY Mellon project was developing was a very busy and critical one for the area, Jack Plumley and for my organization. In addition to the bank project, we were packaging a major expansion with Bus Industries of America and working on a project many, including me, viewed as one that could lead our area in the transformation from what I would call old jobs to the new. As it turned out, that effort tells a very different tale and offers some very different lessons, lessons that should be understood and not forgotten.

Photonics and Politics

Charles E. Franklin had a vision. That vision was to take a new technology and to grow and develop its uses here for the betterment of the nation and our area. Franklin was Colonel Ed Franklin, the head of the Rome Air Defense Center at Griffiss Air Force Base. The new technology was photonics. Photonics most simply put is a communication means by light instead of electricity. Today, it may be best understood by uses as fiber optic cables, laser surgery and the like. In 1987, photonics and its potential uses were in its infancy.

Too few understand that many of the world's most advanced technologies have been developed by the military. And, the United States military has been the most successful military technology developers in history. As noted previously, RADC was an advanced scientific mission at Rome's Griffiss Air Base. One of its small activities in the late 80s was a newly formed Center of Excellence in photonics.

Franklin saw an opportunity to create the framework and structure for a major expansion of this center into a United States Air Force National Photonics Center. He envisioned a new building housing over 400 of the nation's leading experts and support staff in the photonics field to work on defense applications of the technology. Relationships with major universities would be part of the structure. At the same time, he recognized the spin off potential for private business and industry uses which could bring great economic benefit to the central New York region.

Col. Franklin recognized that he needed a special angle to sell the Air Force on his plan. He was bothered by two major potential impediments. The first was the money to create the expanded center; the second, competition from other areas seeking to do the same thing. The two major areas of competition would be Air Force scientific missions in the Boston area and in New Mexico.

Of course, Franklin was not the only Air Force commander who recognized the photonics value and potential.

To help accomplish his goal and to give his plan an edge, he reached out to the political leaders in the community for help. That reach was initially made to Oneida County Executive Jack Plumley and Rome Mayor Carl Eilenberg. Both recognized the tremendous opportunity in the Franklin concept. Plumley for example would come to publically state, "The center would be the greatest economic development opportunity for our area since the digging of the Erie Canal." That conclusion speaks for itself. Both elected officials pledged their support. It was also understood that the creation of a new, advanced scientific mission at Griffiss would help cement the future of both RADC and perhaps the entire base in Rome.

The first meeting with Franklin was attended by Plumley his Planning Director Mike Gapin, Eilenberg and his development director, Ron Conover and Ed Callahan and Ed Ratazzi representing the Rome Chamber and me of the OCIDC. Callahan was the head of the Military Affairs Committee of the Chamber and very tight with Franklin. Callahan was key in structuring the meeting and convincing Franklin of whom to invite. Several basic decisions were made that initial meeting.

The first was that a full development plan had to be created. That plan would be one of the basics—define a building needed in size and location, its cost and its ownership. The matter of how it would be equipped, equipment costs and how that would be financed was also critical. In other words, Franklin's concept had to be put on paper. The second decision was to keep the matter strictly and absolutely confidential until the plan was ready. Franklin wanted everything in order before it went to his superiors.

It was quickly decided that our initial group would be expanded to formulate the actual plan. Several key Franklin people already photonics experts were added to the group. The effort was of the highest priority and a flurry of regular work sessions and meetings took place. Plumley and Eilenberg gave it top priority. Jack and I spoke to Dave Grow and he gave me the authority to devote as much time as necessary on the effort.

What evolved was a plan that created an Air Force and local community partnership to develop the center. The community would build the structure at no cost to the Air Force and the Air Force would finance the research equipment. The building was estimated to cost $18.4 million, the equipment some $30 million. Since the building would not be owned by the Air Force, it would be located off Base. A 22 acre site abutting the base and part of the existing Mohawk Valley Community College area was selected as the site location. A written document was created that outlined the plan and its justification. Franklin presented it up the chain of command. It was OK'd in concept. The matter then became public by choice and necessity.

A Political Train Wreck

Since the building would require what was at the time a sizeable chunk of public money, it became necessary to bring the project into public view. It was decided to zero in on the State of New York as the primary funding source for our share of the plan. I played a fairly significant role in determining that course because of my working relationship with the New York State Urban Development Corporation which was then Governor Mario Cuomo's primary development arm. UDC was the State's counterpart to my organization in the sense that it was a non-profit governed by a business/government mix of board members. I had a very close and successful relationship with UDC's second in command, Lee Webb. We also realized that both the Governor and UDC had placed a high priority on funding high tech projects. My history with UDC going back to the Rome days would not hurt.

Simultaneously, we started briefing state political representatives. Those brought in included the State Senator representing Rome, Nancy Lorraine Hoffman, Rome's Assemblyman, Bill Sears and State Senator Jim Donovan. Donovan was the dean of the local state delegation and thus had the most power. It is important to grasp a bit of these characters in the brewing photonics drama. Hoffman was a real piece of work. She was fairly bright, sharp looking and had an assertive, combative personality. She also had a flair for the dramatic. She was a Democrat. This was viewed as a major plus given Cuomo's party affiliation. Sears was a Republican Assemblyman and as such had no power or influence in the downstate Democrat controlled Assembly. If Hoffman was a piece of work, Donovan was the whole enchilada. He was a tall, John Wayne type figure who was outspoken, gutsy to the extreme and was by that time very powerful in the Republican controlled State Senate. He had received his fame by single handedly holding up the entire state budget process one year over the abortion issue. His one-man filibuster resulted in restrictions on state abortion funding. As Donovan's power grew, so did his hat size. By 1988, he fancied himself as bigger than life. At least that was my impression of him. I had, through the years, dueled with him a few times over minor matters and enjoyed it. I admired his strengths. But, he sure marched to his own beat. This was sometimes helpful; other times destructive.

As we viewed our situation with the state, it looked like a slam dunk. We had an aspiring state Democratic senator who was close to the Governor, a powerful state Republican and a great UDC connection. As a result, it was decided that an effort would be made to include funding for the construction of the center's estimated $18.4 million building cost to be included in the 1988-89 state budget.

All initial meetings both locally and in Albany were extremely positive. The first sign of trouble came directly from Jim Donovan.

In February, Donovan released a public statement questioning the location of the project. He stated his support for its location in Marcy, near the State University. I was told by both parties that this public position was made without Donovan consulting with Plumley or Eilenberg. And, Donovan certainly did not consult with our committee. If he had, he would have learned that the Air Force had an absolute condition that the Center be located on or abutting the Base attached to its commitment for the $30 million in equipment.

For reasons that would defy any logic or grasp of reality, Donovan was simply making a move to try to force locating the Center in his senate district. He had done this with other state facilities before. Perhaps he thought he could move the Air Force on this one. All hell broke loose. Franklin and his people were livid. Hoffman was livid. Sears was livid. The Romans were up in arms. Our committee was both embarrassed and angry. I even issued a public statement saying, "My overall impression is that the Senator is struggling to find ways to be against a tremendous opportunity for the area because it is not in his district." This first show of disunity was to be just the start of one of the most botched efforts in the history of the area.

In a couple of weeks, Donovan threw in the towel on his switch of location attempt and even introduced senate legislation to fund the center with a 50-50, grant/loan. This was followed by a couple of months of political haggling, arguing and chaos. It was sadly typical of Albany political jockeying for position and credit. It started to become obvious to those of us who had worked with the Air Force over the years that the politicians were endangering the project. The Air Force did not like publicity, did not like political disputes and did not like uncertainty. Franklin himself was starting to feel pressure, since both he and those above him believed that the project would be easy to accomplish. They were shocked by the pettiness of the Albany crowd.

Our committee was so alarmed that we issued a statement that said, "We cannot sit idly by and watch this golden economic opportunity slip by because representatives in Albany cannot put the common good above egos and petty jealousies." We wondered if the entire project was in trouble. That question was to be soon answered.

One fateful evening I was swimming laps in the pool at the Rome Family Y. I usually worked out there every evening after work. As I was turning at one point, an arm reached in to grab me. It was a Y staffer telling me that the Mayor of Rome was on the phone and wanted me to rush over to his office. It was just two blocks away. I said to tell the mayor I would as soon as I put some clothes on. When I got to Eilenberg's office, he was there with Ron Conover. They told me that Lee Webb had called and wanted to discuss a message from the governor concerning photonics with us. Lee wanted me on the call. We immediately got excited. Webb had kept plugged into the project and as he had discussed with me and others, was also worried that politics would wreck it. He understood the value of the Photonics Center to the area and to the state.

I called Webb back with the mayor and Ron listening in. Webb had an offer directly from Cuomo. He proposed that UDC loan the entire amount of the building cost to a local entity at a long term, no interest basis. As I recall, the term was to be thirty years. There were two basic conditions to the loan. One was that part of the Center had to include a private business incubator where companies could come in and interact with the Air Force research, thus assisting tech transfer that could hasten civilian business applications of photonics. This was both a reasonable and highly desirable idea and request. Second, he said that UDC would insist that Oneida County guarantee the loan. But, all important, he indicated that it would be a non-recourse guarantee. In other words, the county could not be penalized if repayment wasn't met.

We discussed this condition very carefully. First, if the incubator was in operation, companies would pay rent which would provide a revenue stream. Second, Webb stressed that Cuomo would not support any kind of a grant from anywhere including the state budget. The governor felt that a grant to our project would open the floodgates to high tech grant requests from all over the state that could run into hundreds of millions of dollars. He concluded that a loan/guarantee financing structure would be the only financially feasible route to go.

After a long discussion, we told Webb we liked the offer but had to discuss it with the county executive, who was away. We assured Webb that we would track him down, fill him in and get back to Webb with answer. Plumley was away on hunting or fishing trip. He was contacted and briefed. So was Mike Gapin. It was our consensus that we should take Cuomo's deal. The project had to get done. Whatever, the local obligation assumed; the benefits would far outweigh the debt. Plus, we joked, what would UDC do if we ran into money problems. Many communities were on the hook to the state through UDC or Job Development Authority, or other state entities. This project would leverage $30 million in federal money, high paying jobs that would increase the tax base and perhaps lead to significant private development. And, not to be forgotten, it would strengthen RADC and the base, plus put us on the high tech national, if not world map.

The elected guys were so confident that it could be sold locally that they asked Gapin, Conover and me to meet the next morning to draft a press release announcing the deal. We would coordinate the publicity through Webb. Then someone asked a fateful question? Should we check with Donovan? I think either Plumley or Eilenberg asked it. Jack said he would take care of it. We broke up feeling great. We thought we were about to accomplish one of the most important projects to the future of the area.

Conover, Gapin and I met the following morning in my office at the county airport and started to draft the statement. At some point we were called by Plumley's office and told to put things, "on hold." Several hours later, we were instructed that the deal was off. Senator Donavan said that he had a bipartisan deal in the legislature for the 50-50 grant/loan arrangement. Both Eilenberg and Plumley felt they could not propose the Governor's full loan offer and have Donovan out there saying that he could have secured a $9.2 million grant! Although the three of us sitting in my office instinctively felt something was amiss, we had no choice but to follow instructions.

I can't recall how many days later but on March 29, Donovan publically announced that he was delivering the photonics center funding along the lines of the grant/loan split and that he had a guarantee of approval by the Senate and Assembly! Jack Plumley stated something to the effect that this was a great day for the area. Everyone here thought that Donovan won a better deal. I was bewildered. I wondered how Webb could tell us one thing about Cuomo would live with and Donovan, in effect, the opposite. In New York, nothing got approved in any state budget at any time without the approval of the big three, the Governor, the Senate Majority Leader and the Speaker of the Assembly. I wondered what kind of deal was struck to change Cuomo's mind. My calls to Lee Webb were not returned. I soon learned why.

Almost immediately after Donovan's one man press conference, Mel Miller, the Speaker of the Assembly, issued a public statement calling Jim Donovan, "a liar," saying there was no deal on the project. Miller adamantly said that there would be no money in the budget for the project. On April 14 Donovan acknowledged that there would be no money in the budget for the photonics project and that he would try to revive it under a special funding bill. Cuomo soon stated emphatically that there would be no grant under any circumstance. We were cooked, embarrassed, angry and second guessing ourselves. Lee Webb was upset we told him one thing and did another. He resented our discussing his phone offer with Donovan. The entire effort collapsed under the weight of political grandstanding and high jinks. Cuomo dropped his loan offer. He was pissed, to say the least.

After the debacle, Donovan and others tried to revive the project throughout 1988. It was too late. During that period, the Air Force took a walk from it. Franklin was promoted and reassigned. The state gave lip service to photonics and by the end of the year announced a $100,000 grant to set up a committee and hired an expert to develop photonics tech transfer opportunities. For all of Ed Franklin's vision and hard work we got a paper pushing, talk a lot, do-little committee that lasted for years and accomplished nothing of consequence.

The photonics story is that of an opportunity thrown away by politics at its worst! Is there a bad guy in the story? Were we stupid to not foresee the state path as one of danger? Should we have found ways to do it without even involving the state? These are but a few key questions that can never be answered.

Was Jim Donovan out of control or was he suckered? It was always hard for me to believe that he announced the deal without really believing he had it. Did he so easily get carried away with himself that he tried to force the matter in his John Wayne fashion? Or, was he lied to and then nailed by the Assembly Democrats? I don't know the answer but if Lee Webb could make clear to us that Cuomo would not support a grant; wouldn't it be clear to Donovan? It appeared that Donovan actually thought he could buck Cuomo. Can Eilenberg and Plumley be faulted for listening to Donovan? One would think that they would have understood Albany politics and the Governor's strength, power and ego better. But, most important, should they have understood Donovan's ego better. The answer is that Donovan had boxed in the locals. If they agreed to the Cuomo deal, he would have criticized them soundly and roundly for undermining his "better" deal. Tragically for the area, the only political option was to trust Donovan. That led to his failure but, more importantly, to a major failure for the area and its future.

It is obvious that our area was victimized by politics at its worst. My sense is that we were right in one of our public statements, "Albany cannot put the common good above egos and petty jealousies." To this day, that characteristic remains firmly entrenched in the state capital.

Of the many projects and issues that came up during the Plumley years, two have been presented; one success, one failure. They demonstrate how politics and politicians can help make or break a deal. With the politician, the ego is often a driving force. And most have big ones. That is why it is critical to know how and when to involve them in the business development process. When they control the money, limiting their involvement is impossible. So you live by the political sword or die by it when public money is involved. Jack Plumley did not have a big ego. In the photonics matter he got trapped in an arena he did not control. In the Irving/BNY project it was his arena and he carved out his own role.

Jack left office in 1991, before the end of his term. I label him as a great County Executive in the area of economic development and business understanding. He was from business and knew that better than any county executive in the area's history. He ran a tight ship, was always straight forward and extremely honest. Oneida County prospered under his leadership. OCIDC had a remarkable record of accomplishments. I think the county/OCIDC business development relationship during that period is a model that should be revisited. Overall, there was instability in the county's financial house that Plumley did not solve. Since I was not involved in county government per se, I can't and won't get into them. If, and how much did that have to do with his resignation? I think a lot in the sense that he really got sick of the internal bickering over money and politics. Jack Plumley was succeeded by Raymond Meier.

The Final OCIDC Chapter

Ray Meier was an articulate young attorney who had a Rome political background and served on the Oneida County Board of Legislators. He had a professorial look and mind. I had known him for several years. At one point in the 1980s I had been one of several who met with him to try to convince him to primary Sherry Boehlert for the district's Congressional seat. He didn't bite. Meier was much more of a conservative Republican than Boehlert. As a young man, Meier had worked on the staff of Jim Donovan as well. That brought him close to another attorney and politician from Utica named Bob Julian. Julian was also a County Legislator, in fact the most dominant one. He was the Majority Leader when Meier was voted by the Board to succeed Plumley. Julian himself was bright and articulate but a lot more contentious and controversial than Meier. In fact, Julian could be downright nasty to anyone who disagreed with him. It was rumored that one of the reasons Plumley quit was because he was sick to death of fighting with Julian. But I had always worked well with Julian. He was a strong supporter of my organization. Julian so dominated the Board with his aggressiveness and edge that no one, even Meier, could have been appointed County Executive without his support.

I looked forward to working with Ray. We were conservative philosophical soul mates; he was smart, easy to access and, as Plumley, understood the relationship between government and business. As he often said it was government's role to create a proper business climate and then, get out of the way of private enterprise. Ray was also a member of the McMahon and Grow law firm in Rome. And as mentioned previously, I had worked with Dave Grow in Rome and he was the OCIDC President as Ray assumed the County Executive job. So, the mix could not be better. If I could ever have thought our relationship with the County Executive could have improved over that with Jack, the thought would have occurred with the Meier appointment.

That judgment proved to be right. The three years in which Ray was County Executive and I staff head of OCIDC were both extremely productive and enjoyable. There are a couple of important aspects of my recollections of the Meier era that proved to be of great importance to the area. A look into them in some detail will result in some interesting lessons for the area and to set the historical record straight in more detail than has been previously publicized.

1992 Sales Tax Hike

As an interim County Executive, Meier operated under Jack Plumley's last budget during the remainder of 1991. As he functioned in office and prepared for his own budget, he concluded that the County was operating under a systemic deficit that was $9 million and growing. The solution to overcoming the debt and balancing the budget favored by Ray, his staff and some legislators was to increase the County's then 7% sales tax. Since I was not a county employee nor worked with the Executive's office and legislature on anything other than economic development matters, I was not involved in County budget matters. So, I can't judge nor reference the initial sales tax increase direction. As most citizens who were aware of what was going on, I did grasp that county spending and taxation policies were growing, to a large extent because of various federal and state mandates. Those mandates contributed to an exploding social service burden.

To implement a sales tax increase, Meier needed to jump two hurdles. The first was to receive County Board legislative approval; the second to receive State legislative approval. Neither was considered a sure thing. The primary issue affecting both the political support and ultimately the public support was the determination of how proceeds from the hike would be split between the county, towns and cities. In other words, if the tax was to be hiked votes had to be bought to a certain extent. There were two chances of passing the hike without settling this question; the proverbial slim and none. Sure enough quickly after the County Executive submitted his increase proposal in early January of 1992, question of the split and support arose on both levels. The first step was to settle the issue at the county board level from which it could be submitted to the state. Simultaneously two area state legislators, State Senator Bill Sears and Assemblyman Ralph Eannace made it clear that they would not support enabling legislation unless and until a revenue sharing plan was part of the County legislation. Sears represented Rome area interests; Eannace Utica. At the same time, Bob Julian was dead set on securing extra money for his home city, Utica. This whole pattern was a lesson in parochialism. Instead of recognizing and supporting an overall need to solve a county wide problem, everyone wanted a piece of the action. This also meant the increase itself would have to be larger. For, several other issues were in play.

Adding fuel to the fire was the financial troubles both cities were in. For example, Utica's mayor, Lou LaPolla was staring a 40% property tax increase in the face and was desperate for money. There were also town pressures.

New Hartford, the area's largest town and an ever growing commercial center expected more sales tax money since the town felt it was the primary source of it. So, Meier was having trouble putting a deal together. He called on me to help define the problem and arbitrate a political settlement. Why me?

I think that he concluded that an outside, objective view would help elevate the process from politics. He also knew that OCIDC had built an outstanding rapport with both the legislators and the city mayors. And, I assume he respected our competency. We decided to help under a couple of conditions. One, that my board president, Dave Grow, approve. Two, that anything OCIDC did be confidential and finally, that I involve our top finance guy, Dave Leffert, to assist. The confidential part was important since OCIDC was both non-partisan and non-political. With a wink from Grow, we did not think it wise to even inform our board of directors that we were getting involved. Leffert was needed because as a trained accountant with a long track record, he understood numbers much better than I. And, I wanted to understand the county's financial position as a first step. After all, we couldn't argue for something unless we truly understood the problem and need. Meier also appreciated outside, non-political affirmation of his conclusions concerning the county's financial condition.

After some intensive research on our part, we concluded that Meier's deficit alarm was accurate. Soon thereafter, off hour meetings were held on a Saturday and Sunday morning to try to hack out an agreement under which all parties could support. Participating were the reps from the County Board that represented both rural and urban interests, the Republican and Democrat leadership and representatives from Utica and Rome. LaPollla himself represented Utica while Joe Griffo, the Rome mayor sent staff. I was struck by a couple of things, the first being the turn-out. That itself signaled a willingness to deal. The second was that all agreed not to publicize the meeting thus eliminating grandstanding. It was also clear that Julian was to dominate the discussion.

The meetings were extremely low key and civil. Enough progress was made on Saturday to justify the Sunday morning meeting at which agreement was reached. There was no controversy whatsoever of the County's financial plight and general understanding that a sales tax hike was preferable to that of a property tax increase. The fundamental position of Meier was that the bulk of the additional revenue had to retire the County debt and to build up a fund surplus to assure holding the line on property taxes for a three year period. LaPolla was arguing strongly throughout that Utica deserved more of a split than was being discussed. His position was that his city bore the brunt of the area's social problems and costs and of government and non profit tax exempt properties.

The deal struck was that of the $18 million in new revenue, projected to be generated by a 1% tax increase, $2.3 million would go to Utica, $1.3 to Rome and $2 million to be shared among the towns. That left $12 million for the county. LaPolla was not pleased but decided to go along with it anyway. Once the arrangement was acted upon in the form of formal County Board legislation on March 31, 1992, LaPolla made the public statement that he, "reluctantly" supported it. No mention was made by anyone of the secret meetings held that resulted in the final package. No mention was made of the "real" issue that was present right along. That centered on the question of why 1% and not more. The answer was pretty simple. Ray Meier was not crazy about raising the tax in the first place. In fact he has been quoted to say that he considered raising the percentage as a "low" point in his years as County Executive. After all, he was a conservative and as such philosophically against raising taxes in the first place. He was not about to raise the sales tax more than the 1% and have Oneida County become the area with the highest sales tax in the State.

This author makes three observations stemming from that experience. Elected leaders of various stripes with different constituencies came together to work out a solution to an important problem. And, they did so in private. There was no posturing or finger pointing. The leadership of all those involved, particularly Meier and Julian was clearly exhibited as was LaPolla's, who was under severe public fire over his own budget difficulties. He did not allow this to poison the well of the County situation and did compromise. One might argue that beggars can't be choosy but I viewed LaPolla's conduct as a major plus. Of course it can also be argued that politicians can always get together on receiving more revenue. Taxing is often easier than cutting costs.

The second is the reaffirmation of the fact of life that once government gets more money it will spend it, and more. Meier's action did balance the budget and created a surplus. His successors spent that and more. The County sales tax and property taxes have continued to rise along with spending. The increase was sold publically as temporary; to solve onetime crises. Temporary became permanent. Eventually, Oneida County was to have the highest sales tax rate in the entire State of New York. Ironically it was imposed by Joe Griffo who later became county executive with Ray Meier's support. As we've seen and continue to see on levels of government in New York and Washington, spending and taxation tend to have a never ending life cycle. Very few elected officials have halted or slowed this pattern. One time justifications for tax increases have a way of becoming repeated. And, utilizing a sales type tax as a revenue source is one politicians love since the consumer does not notice it. It is a hidden tax and, therefore, more insidious than other forms.

Third, one idea of Meier's that got lost in the shuffle as this issue was being debated was that of using some of the funds for the study of governmental consolidation. For a time, he proposed that $2 million of the new revenue be set aside and used to study and recommend basic structural change, consolidation of services that would deal with the fiscal future of the area's local government structure. As entities rushed in to get their hands on short term funds, longer term questions quickly and silently fell by the wayside.

Visionaries going way back to the 1960's recognized that a governmental arrangement made in the 18th and 19th centuries could not efficiently serve modernity. One of these visionaries was Dr. Virgil Crisafulli of Utica College who wrote of and recommended consolidated government. Meier was on the same wave length some thirty years later. I think he was smart enough to realize that his particular fix at the time would be not only temporary but that a more radical structural change was necessary. The financial problems of today make those of 1992 look like chump change. What might have been if the consolidation pot of money was put into place? That will never be known. What is known is that seventeen years have passed and that no dramatic and necessary change has been achieved. The Utica-Rome area is still operating under an archaic government system. And, it continues to pay a steep price for it. It could be argued that it has reached the tipping point; that the proverbial water out of a stone situation now exists. Taxes climb, people and jobs leave and incomes fall while the structures of government remain unchanged. This is an unsustainable situation that confronts the area as this book is being written.

A Big Victory

In March of 1993, the area was still in the midst of one of its harshest winters. The snow was piled three feet high and it was freezing. Weather was not the only concern in the area. There were also fears that the local economy was also heading for the deep freeze. The possibility of Griffiss being on a new base closing list arose and there was worry of the buyout of GE's defense operations by Martin-Marietta. Both could result in major local job cuts. Some even feared losing all of what was left of GE in Utica.

Unknown to all but a few, work had been started four months earlier on an opportunity that could give the area a major economic boost. The story of this opportunity merits telling.

In August of 1992, our office received a blind lead from the New York State Commerce Department. They were assisting an unidentified Fortune 500 company identify possible development sites in Central New York. The site had to be a minimum of 200 acres. That was a large site. In fact, there was no site that large in our existing inventory of land that we or other industrial development or municipal entities in Oneida County controlled or listed.

I met with my staff, Joe Karam, the person in charge of our site inventory list and our new marketing director, Christine Powroznik to discuss the inquiry. Yes, Karam was the same Joe from the Assaro days. I had recommended his hiring to our Board in the mid eighties and they went along with the recommendation. And, as he had done to Dick Assaro, he drove me crazy most of the time. But, he was a friend and had his moments of genius. Chris was a very smart, attractive young lady who was over qualified for the job. She had returned here to assist her ailing mother. OCIDC experienced good fortune to have her available and interested in coming aboard. My good fortune was even better since we eventually married. The three of us jumped into responding to the request.

As we looked at the inquiry we came up with three sites. One was a site in Rome the RIDC could marshal if necessary, one the privately owned land across from our industrial park in Whitestown and the third a privately owned site in Marcy. That 230+ acre site was owned by a local businessman named Lou Leogrande who I had known slightly over the years and who Joe knew well. The package we quickly submitted included the details of these sites and a complete demographic/labor analysis of the area that was part of our standard marketing package that Chris compiled and used for prospects. We weren't terribly excited since the so-called, blind, big inquiries usually didn't amount to much. In this instance, we were wrong. This was to amount to a very big deal.

We were pretty bummed out when we learned that a site selection specialist wanted to physically review the sites on Labor Day, a day we had off. Who was willing to work? Karam volunteered to show him around. I sure agreed to let him since I had my heart on playing golf. I guess it was my Slavic nature that made me feel guilty, but when the day came, I decided to meet Joe and the site analyst at their first stop. I left for the site without telling Joe I was coming. When I arrived at the meeting location, I almost died. There in all his overweight splendor stood Joe in cut-off shorts and tee shirt. What an image! I guess Joe had thought day off, holiday clothes would somehow be appropriate. I dispatched him home to change and took over. He rejoined us later. The site analyst was alone and would identify his client. We hit it off very well and had a long, productive day. After his visit, he called several times for more information. Only then did we start to get excited.

In October, we learned, from the State and the site selection specialist that the client was Walmart. And the company was looking for a site for their first Northeastern distribution center. Upstate New York was in the running. We were one of several possible locations. The contest was on! We then informed Dave Grow, OCIDC President and Ray Meir of Walmart's interest. Obviously, they both pledged full support. Both were sworn to secrecy.

Most companies hate publicity prior to their decisions being made. This was described in the Met Life project description. In Walmart's case, the hate was doubled since they had a huge distrust of both government and unions. They wanted no up-front, premature publicity. In fact, the first Walmart guy I spoke with over the phone said that if any news leaked, we could kiss them goodbye. This was no idle threat. Dave and Ray understood this very clearly. As the three of us discussed the client and the project the decision was made not to discuss it with our respective boards. No chances of political grandstanding or loose talk of any kind were to be taken.

The project really heated up when Lee Scott and his team of four or five Walmart engineering types flew in to look at sites and to tour the area. At that time, Scott was the head of Walmart's entire distribution network. He would make the recommendation that would count. Years later, he would become the CEO of the entire company. The bad news was that Scott wasn't limiting his trip to one area. Sites in the Albany-Amsterdam area were on his schedule.

We organized a two car caravan to transport the Walmart team. When they landed, I was struck by a number of things. Scott himself was a relatively young, good looking guy dressed informally in an aviator's jacket. He was instantly nice, friendly and exhibited a good knowledge of the area that went beyond the information we had been providing. He told me quickly as I drove him that he had been reading local papers for quite some time. He was yet another company head from the outside that looked at areas way beyond business type reports. Politicians, media outlets and people in general don't understand that they are often being watched in this way and can assist or screw up a project by questionable behavior and poor public statements. Scott made comments that he assessed our county government as, conservative, which he viewed as a big positive. He knew who Ray Meier was by name. The other interesting aspect of the tour was that Scott was intensely interested in the development sites and even more in other aspects of the community. The fact that Chris, who was charged with organizing the nuts and bolts of the tour, included facilities like Murnane, now Donovan, Field, the Memorial Parkway with its unique inner city ski tow and beautiful residential areas turned out to be extremely important. Lee was not only interested in community characteristics as a way of judging what we were all about but he knew he would be sending key corporate people to live, work and visit here should Walmart invest here. So, things like a kid's ability to play and see baseball here were important to him. A nice house in a decent neighborhood with good schools was of prime importance. He stressed the Walmart family philosophy and concerns. They would only send their people to communities that supported family life. In her research and due to her past financial background working for large investment houses, Chris nailed the "family" concept key to Walmart and tailored part of the tour to it.

As with the Irving people and other prospects and clients not covered in detail in this book, we had the feeling that we hit it off with Scott. One dictum of his office prior to his trip was that he wanted no publicity and he did not want to meet politicians. I think he equated the two. A couple of important factors did arise on the spot relating to the possible site for the project. First, they really zeroed in on the River Road site in Marcy for one obvious reason; it was closest to the New York State Thruway. Since the project was a distribution center, the truck/highway relationship was of obvious and paramount importance. One logistical problem was that there was no road connector between the site and the major local highway, Rt. 49. And, Rt. 49 was the main route to the interstate. Recognizing that County Executive Meier had pledged to assist the project in any way, we assured Scott that a connector solution could be found. There was also a problem with a section of Rt. 49 passing through a small local road section. In other words, the highway was not a straight shot to the Thruway. Scott did not view this as a deal breaker but did want some sort of handle on when the highway tie in would be completed. As he departed, he gave us a very firm indication that we were serious contenders for the project and that the team that would be doing the follow up work with us would soon contact us. We were both pleased and confident. We got to work.

The Walmart team was headed by Matt Cima from the Bentonville corporate headquarters working with engineers from a Texas based consulting firm. That firm was used by Walmart in site selection and development projects all over the country. Their lead guy was named Ken. I can't recall his last name but I do recall his Texas twang and extremely pleasant personality. When their team first came in to meet with us, I was struck by three features. They were as smart and well organized as any group of professionals I had ever met. They were extremely serious in business matters and nice and very funny to hang with after hours. Ken could take your head off in a meeting and have you in stitches having a beer after work. Walmart forced them to stay at Motel 6 and rent small, cheaper cars. We constantly ribbed them about their tiny cars and dumpy rooms. We tried to make up for their discomfort by treating them to great dinners. We were experiencing firsthand experience with Walmart's attention to the bottom line. Their people sure did not travel first class but their profits and stock price did. Sadly, I did not buy it on the spot.

It took several trips and meetings for their team to examine the area, the site and to work carefully with us to very specifically and bluntly tell us what Walmart expected in order for us to land the project. The list was long and complicated all building to meeting Walmart's ambitious opening target day. If they were not confidant that all details and commitments could be met on time, we would not get the project. Without getting into a boring checklist of issues, it should be obvious to the reader as it was to us that organizing a 230 acre, 1 million square foot project on a privately owned site requiring new roadways, complicated property purchases, permits, hearings and tax agreements along with a host of other issues, some even unknown, would be a monumental task for us. And, it all had to be started with no press leaks. Walmart did not want publicity until they were ready to announce.

In January of 1993, a confidential meeting was held, hosted by OCIDC, with our President, Dave Grow, Ray Meier, Bob Julian and Walmart's team. From that meeting flowed the decision to create a large local "project team" consisting of representatives of all agencies and municipalities who needed to be involved in the project. Meier and Julian were to take care of assuring that all involved would be sworn to secrecy. Julian was to inform trusted members of the county Board of the effort. Our staff and the Oneida County Planning Department would coordinate the entire effort. Mike Gapin would assign his top guy, John Kent, to work on the project with us virtually full time. Simultaneously, OCIDC would work to coordinate land purchase details with Lou Leogrande and Walmart. In this vein, the long time personal relationships we had, particularly Joe Karam's with Lou would prove to be very helpful. As we brought him into the discussions, the fact that Lou was a pure businessman also helped. I must also add that he exhibited a strong sense of what the project would mean to the area. He understood all aspects of the deal, its importance and the need to keep matters confidential. Things were starting to move rapidly and positively.

Our project team consisted of my staff, John Kent and Gapin, key Town of Marcy officials led by Brian Scala, the Supervisor, State Labor reps, State DOT, Bob Julian, Assemblywoman Roann Destito and Ray Meier. Destito was included because the site was in her district and the Governor was a Democrat. We did not include any Republican state reps. The local Republican leaders pledged to handle them. The Photonics debacle was not to be repeated. At the first organizational meeting it was decided that I would chair the group and that we would meet weekly until every task we had to do got done. This turned out to be a remarkable process in many ways.

The most striking feature was that with the mix of government staffers, town types and elected politicians not one word of what we were doing ever leaked to the press. There is one aspect of the secrecy that was kind of funny. Over a time at OCIDC I and my staff had developed a close relationship with reporter named Robbie Duchow. Rob worked at the Rome Daily Sentinel. Whenever I could, I gave Rob some early word on projects so he could scoop the OD. I so disliked the Utica Observer Dispatch in those days that I took pleasure in that little game I played with Rob. Consequently Rob used to hang around our office and call a lot. He started to smell something big going on during this sensitive period. The name Walmart actually came up. Even before the distribution center project came up as a lead, Walmart had been working with a retail developer to locate a store in the area. By the time we were working quietly on the distribution project, the retail division of Walmart was working on a controversial project in New Hartford. So, when Rob started to hint that he was hearing about a Walmart project, we simply told him that it must involve the New Hartford store project. He bought it. The two did intersect at one time. It's another interesting story.

One of the pleasures of my life since high school was to play poker. While at OCIDC, I sat in on a game with a bunch of friends every late Friday afternoon at the Elks Club in Utica. We would come in around 4, play until 7 and then head home or go out with our wives to dinner. One Friday about six o'clock the Elk's bartender came into the room to tell me I had an important phone call. I reluctantly got up to take it after he reiterated that sounded like a really important call. When I picked up the phone in the bar, the caller identified himself as Cy Young from Walmart. Initially, I thought it was a joke since the only Cy Young I ever heard of was the baseball Cy Young. I did not know of the first name spelling difference. He convinced me it wasn't a joke and issued a threat to me. He said that we would not get the distribution project unless I and my organization helped him get his retail store in New

Hartford. I was stunned. No one from Walmart had ever to that point linked the two. The call also screwed up my poker game. I don't think that I argued with Young on the phone but I did not appreciate being threatened. I left the game and called Matt Cima, to find out what in hell was going on.. He knew Young but knew nothing about the call. He promised to talk to Lee Scott on Monday and get back to me. He did and informed me that Young was censured for making that call and quoted Scott as saying that the distribution center project had nothing to do with the retail one. I never heard from Young again. Walmart did soon get the go ahead for the super center; without my help.

Another feature of the local project team was how professional everyone was. I don't think that any area could muster a better group. Matt and/or Ken sat in on many of our meetings on Walmart's behalf and they indicated that our team gave them the confidence that we could deliver. They endorsed us as the best local group they had worked with to date. That meant so much coming from them and who they represented.

I'm not sure that the area ever had its act together in better fashion. The only thing that comes close is the effort that saved RADC covered earlier in this book.

It soon became impossible to keep the project a secret. Either in late February or early March we appeared at meetings of both the Republican and Democrat county legislature caucuses to discuss the project. We needed assurance from the County that it would fund the building of that connecter road linking the Marcy site to Route 49We also had to touch base with then Congressman Sherry Boehlert to come up with a reasonable estimate of when Federal monies would be available to complete the linking of Route 49 to the Thruway. Remember, Walmart required those answers. Shortly after those meeting and conversations both Ray Meier and I started getting phone calls from reporters and others about a big Walmart project. We decided that we had to go public. By then, which was mid March, we knew that we were the selected location for the project barring any unforeseen problems. We conferred with Walmart about publicity. They gave the go ahead for us to announce the project. They would not affirm or confirm it publically but would very soon be ready to formally start applying for building permits. They were simply not into the pr game. Of course, Ray understandably was. He was a politician and was playing the key political role in the project.

On March 19, he and I held a press conference announcing that Oneida County would be the home of a 1million square foot Walmart distribution center that upon opening would employ 700-800 jobs and soon after those 1,000 jobs. Not long after, Walmart did start the permit processes thus confirming our press announcement. We won the project! Although we would work hard and long to assist the project with the town, state and other agencies and people, our real work was accomplished in winning the project. Or, so we thought. Even though several aspects of the construction like site clearance and the acquisition of property through which the connector would be built, the project was threatened on two fronts that summer.

It was discovered along the way that the sheer size of the building, 1million sq. feet and the cookie cutter Walmart design did not meet a provision of a New York State building code as it related to fire safety exits. A variance would be required. The only group that could grant such a variance was a special fire safety group operating out of Albany. They were private fire types appointed by the governor. There were three major problems. We were too late to get on their summer meeting agenda, at least one member was from an area that had been a rival of ours for the project and the board was hard assed about granting variances. All this meant that we not only could lose precious time but could lose the project. Walmart could not nor would not change their design. It was their way or no way!

We moved on two fronts. First, the Marcy and Oneida County volunteer fire groups helped immeasurably to show and to testify that the building lay out was safe for employees and that there was plenty of assurance both by design and Walmart's tremendous safety training that a major fire could not start and that employees could exit easily if any kind of fire did start. The group of firemen that helped us blew my socks off with their expertise and their willingness to write a report and give oral testimony.

Ray Meier and Roann Destito led the effort to bring both sides of the aisle of Albany politics to bear on the board to both insert us on the summer agenda and to grant the variance. Every politician who could help was enlisted.

We got the meeting and made the presentation. When one of the Governor's top people, the Secretary of State, walked in and stood in the back of the room to observe, we knew the variance was locked. She would not have been there otherwise. Walmart got the variance. The project was a go, again, so we thought.

An Odd Final Roadblock

In August of 1993, a legal dispute arose that threatened the entire project and the jobs it would bring. Preliminary site work and road work was already underway when a really strange claim was made. We the Industrial Development Corporation and our sister agency, the Oneida County Industrial Development Agency were threatened with a law suit. To understand the threat, one must first understand the ownership and development process. It is quite technical.

The OCIDA was a financing arm the OCIDC used to assist development projects. It issued revenue bonds that were tax exempt. Companies who were involved in expansion projects creating new jobs could apply for this bond financing to fund their project. The advantage would be tax breaks in both sales tax relating to construction materials purchased and in local property taxes. In place of normal property taxes, the bond mechanism set up a payment in lieu of system under which the developing company would receive limited abatement over a set period of time. On both sales and. property tax costs, large projects benefitted significantly. This bond mechanism had Federal legislative underpinnings and all communities used the mechanism to attract projects. In other word, Walmart would have gotten the same incentives at any location. To receive the benefits, the property had to be owned by the OCIDA. What was set up was a sale, lease back arrangement under which Walmart deeded the property to us and we long term leased it back to the company. Under the lease, they retained all rights and obligations the same as if they owned it. The OCIDC staff was the staff to the OCIDA and several people, including Dave Grow, were board members of both.

So, as owners of the Walmart site we were sued by Charles Gaetano and Mona Caruso. Gaetano was the head of a large local construction company and Caruso a local businesswoman. They jointly owned land called Bergamo East which was located north of the Walmart site.

Their suit which was filed at the New York State Supreme Court level claimed that they had right of way rights through our site involving a 1.6 acre strip of land running through the site that contained a sewer line that served their land. Since the Walmart project would go right over this strip therefore making it defunct, they were claiming millions of dollars of financial damages.

We were stunned for a number of reasons. First, there was never any indication of any kind that the right of way existed to begin with. Second, when we and the County Planners rushed out to find the sewer, we found that it was broken, had been broken for a very long period of time and was not being used for anything or

politics. Both wound up having very successful judicial careers. Cardamone rose to the Federal bench retiring one notch below the US Supreme Court level. I often wondered how the area would have evolved if one or both of these men sought regular political office or even just kept Republican control. Tenney in particular would seemingly have had a tremendous political future. He was tall, handsome, witty and articulate. In my opinion, he chose the smarter route. I wonder if he ever regretted it. I know Dick Cardamone did not since he was far less comfortable as a political person than was Tenney. He was a sharp, always the politician judge. The politician in him was to try to make both sides happy.

On the second day of the trial, I was called as a witness. To this day, I don't understand why. The breaking point occurred when Pratt approached, looked at me squarely in the eye and asked in dramatic fashion, "Is it not true that in the past, the army used my clients land?" I responded, "Yes, I think that is true". Pratt turned his back and walked away. As he neared his desk, he whipped around and his voice thundered, "And, what army was that?" I looked up at him and said, "Why, I guess it was the United States Army; I think that's the only army we have." The court again erupted in laughter. We had learned that back in World War II, the land had been used for army barracks and training. Whatever that had to do with anything escaped me and the judge.

Well, Tenney had had enough. He ordered everyone into his chambers. As we sat down, he said, "If anyone things that I'm going to rule in a way that costs this community 800 jobs, they are crazy. I am not going to jeopardize Walmart in any way." He then went on to say that the matter would be settled in the following way. That should Bergamo East ever be developed to the point of requiring sewers, a new line would be put in the roadway right of way. At that time, the cost of the sewer line which was estimated to be $218,000 would be shared by the Bergamo East owners and my corporation. He said, we'd all better agree or he would be very upset. I quickly excused myself to call Dave Grow to discuss the settlement with him. We agreed that we should take the deal, get the matter over and that $108,000, as distasteful as it was, was not a huge deal compared to a possible delayed or lost Walmart project. The matter was settled. As of this writing, nothing has ever been developed on the Bergamo East property. The Walmart distribution center sits there as the largest building in Oneida County and employs over 1,000 people. It has been tremendous boon to the area in employment, investment and in support of civic charities.

A Goodbye Cheer

By the following spring, I was eager to leave the Industrial Development Corporation. The primary reason was 15 years. I had never been in one job anywhere near that long. I was also itching to jump into the private sector and to take a shot at making a lot more money. Although I was paid decently where I was, I was never going to get rich there. And, when I turned 50, I realized my good years were limited. I also thought that bad local economic times could be on the way. Griffiss was due to get realigned and closed and GE was again rumored to be in trouble in Utica. After Walmart, I sensed there was no place to go but down at OCIDC.

That winter, I discussed my interest in a job change with my friend Dominic Chang. He had left Irving Trust months after it was taken over by the Bank of New York. He didn't like the new bank's culture and was also driven to be in business for himself. Even while a bank employee, Dominic had side businesses and was, at heart, the classic entrepreneur. He and another former Irving banker had left the bank to start a company called Family Golf Centers. The company was built and was building year round covered golf driving and practice ranges in the New York City metropolitan area. They were doing gangbusters. Their first facility on Long Island was making millions and they were rapidly developing more. Dominic told me not to do anything without before checking with him. I assured him I was just in the preliminary stage of my thinking and exploration.

As spring of 1994 approached, he called and said that he was working on a project that he would want me to run. He was putting things together and wanted me to visit him to discuss a job change. At the same time, some leadership changes were being made at the OCIDC. The most important was that Dave Grow was stepping down. Sitting in on meetings with a Board committee formed to recommend Dave's successor, the bet was that it would be the president of a local bank named Bill Schrauth. I didn't say a word given my urge to leave, but over the years that I knew him, I never warmed up to Schrauth. I found him to be an all talk, no action kind of guy. So, when the call came from Dominic I was more than ready to talk. By then, Chris and I had been married for about a month which was also creating some office difficulties as far as my board was concerned. They were wrong but as the saying goes, perception is everything. In fact, the office was never functioning more smoothly.

Chris and I went to meet with Chang at one of his company's locations. I was blown away by the golf center. I had never seen anything of its kind, a doubled tiered, enclosed, heated driving range with a full pro shop, great mini-golf area, packed with people in the middle of the day. Dominic wanted me to join the company and to develop his company's first upstate New York project. He wanted to build a center of the type we were in plus a golf dome facility for winter use. He thought the Syracuse area would be the best to start. He explained "just to start" as meaning the first of many in upstate and other colder climate areas. He wanted me to be the head of what the company would call its Northern District. I would be the regional director and be designated a corporate Vice President. Most important, he explained that in the near future it was his goal to take the company public and that I would be, along with others, awarded stock opportunities. In the meantime Family Golf would match my OCIDC salary. We told him that we would discuss it at home and get back to him. By the time we got home, we had decided to take his offer. I wanted to gamble on the change. The upside made the gamble worth the risk. We had no major financial obligations of a serious nature. The bottom line was that I liked and had a lot of faith in Dominic and his personal integrity and financial abilities. The fact that his old boss and my friend, Jim Ganley the other ex Irving guy we worked so closely with was on the company's Board of Directors did not hurt. I was convinced that I could make a pile of money and have a great time doing it with these guys. The time arrived to plunge into the biggest career gamble since I cast my fate with the Assaro group. It was interesting that Assaro and Chang shared the same first name in pronunciation and that both loomed so large in my life.

I called Dominic back the next day and accepted his offer. We formulated a time for the switch. He asked me if I could remain at OCIDC to until the fall and perhaps use some vacation time to start investigating the Syracuse project. That would both save Family Golf money and allow me to transition professionally from OCIDC. We agreed.

By late September, I made it public that I was leaving in October. My last week on the job, I received a call from Larry Mahoney. Larry was the head of the new Walmart distribution center which had recently opened. I thought to myself, "Please let this not be a major problem to spoil my final week." I took Chris with me since she had been in charge of coordinating all of Walmart's pre opening issues including the very important and complicated training programs assisting the company. Larry greeted us and ushered us into their huge assembly area. The hundreds of new employees were all there and proceeded to give me the Walmart cheer. I was the "squiggle." I could think of no better way to end that chapter of my life.

A Look Back at County Leadership

I recall talking about the County Executive's job one afternoon with Jack Plumley. Jack made the point that the overwhelming part of the County budget is comprised of Social Services and Public Works. And, other than appointing people the County Executive does not have much to say or to do with running those functions. So much of Social Services is mandated by Federal and State law while highways get plowed, cleaned, maintained and paved pretty much as a matter of course by people and processes that have functioned for decades. So, on paper the job of the County Executive is a piece of cake. But, there is much more than what is on paper. To offer insight from the perspective I had working with county executives, it's best to start with some political features of Oneida County government.

The most striking feature of Oneida County government has been its one party dominance. Since the executive form of government was adopted in Oneida County in 1960, 49 years before the writing of this book, there has only been one elected Democrat county executive, Bill Bryant. And he did not complete two full terms. So, what started out as a reform effort, that of amending the county charter to bring about progressive change, resulted in one party controlling the top county elected position for 44 of 49 years. I don't think that this one party control was either envisioned or desirable in some pretty significant ways. For, as pointed out in an earlier chapter, the charter change to begin with was inspired by the goal to rid the county of the Harold Kirch single party, boss style machine.

The legislative branch of the government has been in Republican control for the full 49 years! In the legislature, the majority so dominated over the years that the minority basically threw in the sponge and, in effect, joined as one. The long time Minority Leader, Harry Hertline, was described by most Republicans as being a more reliable vote than some of the Republican members. It is clear that the longer the Republican control remained, Democrats accepted patronage, projects and service attention in trade for, playing ball.

The one party control is somewhat understandable given the Republican voter registration edge in the county. But, even with that edge, such extended dominance cannot easily be rationalized as truly democratic. Republican leadership both inside and outside of county government should be credited with the political acumen of building and maintaining a powerful political machine. This was accomplished as all political machines are through patronage, money raising, contract and purchasing favoritism and the host of normal political strategies. Also, all media outlets, particularly those of the newspapers, have historically treated county government with kid gloves insofar as investigating its performance and characteristics.

In Rome, this is very understandable given the fact that virtually all major county government leadership has come from Rome. The *Rome Sentinel* has and is owned by a Rome based family that is fiercely parochial. The paper surely has understood that the Rome area over the years has received far more from county government than it demographically deserved. The Utica newspaper, not locally owned seemed to historically concentrate more on city politics. And, as time wore on since the late 1950s lessened its investigative journalism across the board. By and large, the papers have given county government a free pass from extensive, detailed investigative reporting.

It is clear that one-party dominance has not been healthy for the people of the county. Some of the reasons will be addressed as it relates to the county executive position and to those executives I have written about. But, overall, the fact that Oneida County government has in practices, programs and employees, not changed in any significant way in nearly fifty years is an important contributor to the area's decline. Modern technology has not been employed, political boundaries not altered or consolidated, budgets not properly and comprehensively scrutinized and "new blood and brains" not recruited. This business as usual approach has produced a stale government absent of innovation, creativity and change. It has also created political cronyism and financial waste.

One could argue convincingly that the voter has simply received what has been voted for. That argument will be dealt with more extensively in the book's final chapter. The argument itself is interesting and always present in our democratic system in all areas on all levels. Does reelection mean satisfaction or are the advantages of incumbency so significant that unseating any incumbent is extremely difficult?

It is interesting to note that as this book is being written, the Republican machine in Oneida County shows signs of wearing out as all machines do. Their hold on the Executive's chair and decision making seems to be weakening. There are three primary reasons for this growing change. First, and in my estimation most important, population demographics have changed and continue to change. Since 1995, the area has lost about 20,000 people, a staggering amount for an area the size of Oneida County. Most of this loss has come from middle management type people resulting from the loss of particular industries such as GE/Martin Marietta and from the loss of most of Griffiss Air Force Base. More will be added later in this book, but in the context of this section, these people tended to be Republicans. So, party registration numbers have tightened in that period. Second, most of in-migration has come from Russian, Bosnian, Latino, Asian, and African immigrants who, if they become citizens and register to vote tend to register and vote Democrat. Finally, the old, inbred nature of the

Republican machine has turned away new, young blood. Many younger people interested in politics who ideologically think like Republicans and might have even been registered as Republicans have switched parties as the result of being unwelcomed by Republican relics.

Another aspect of the long Republican rule directly relates to the county executive position and to those executives with whom I worked. Allow me to start with a few preliminary comments. During my tenure as the Executive Vice President of the Oneida County Industrial Development Corporation, all levels of county government, Executives, Legislators and staffs were supportive of me and my organization. This was a major accomplishment given the divisions and disappointments of previous years. Of course, business growth benefits all and maintaining good relationships is not difficult if one is producing. It was also our practice to put deals together and then give the politicians their due which as I've described was earned by them. Sherry Boehlert, Jack Plumley and Ray Meier were from my perspective all good men. Jack and Ray were bright in more ways than Boehlert but he was the political genius of the three. That political genius ultimately earned him over 20 years in the Congress of the United States. He could be all things to all people which made for a good candidate, but a poor leader. Strong leaders do not always bend with the political winds.

One example of several was Boehlert's positions on abortion. When he first ran for office for county executive and then Congress, he courted the Conservative Party for endorsements. He professed to be pro-life. After becoming secure in his Congressional seat, he became pro-abortion. He then courted democrats and pro-abortion campaign contributions as he evolved into Mr. Republican Moderate. Now, one can understand a legitimate switch from pro-choice to pro-life on both scientific and moral terms. I can think of no reason for a pro-life to pro-abort switch except political. I suspect Sherry was always pro-choice but postured to the right when he felt it expedient. In fact, in all the years I knew him, I felt he would have been a Democrat except for the knowledge that being a Republican was a surer path to political success here.

This long term, under scrutinized Republican control of the government meant that the party, its leaders and its candidates could pretty much do as they pleased. In that sense, the county executive's job was used as a stepping stone by Boehlert and Meier. Both had political ambitions that did not end at being county executive. Boehlert had a near life time ambition to become "the Congressman," while Meier recognized the job's intellectual and practical limitations from the outset. Both, therefore, served only briefly. Plumley was more home grown and content politically. I viewed him as the best of group as it related to business development. All were gentlemen. Jack was the strongest in certain ways. One little story illustrates my point.

A local businessman had started a company and came to us for financial help. Our first staff meeting with him was rocky. He was under the impression that his words of promises and plans should have been enough for us to write him a check on the spot. Of course, we had both the fiduciary responsibility and wherewithal to demand much more, like a full business plan. He did not appreciate our requirements. Not too long after, I received a call from Plumley's office asking if I could attend a meeting in Jack's office at which this businessman would be present. We met. The first words out of this guys mouth was a threat to, "go to the paper" if we did not help him. Jack promptly stood back up and in a red faced fashion threw the guy out of the office stating that we don't deal with anyone who makes threats. I can't imagine Boehlert or Meier handling the situation that way. Interestingly, this guy did go into that business. The business failed.

The other characteristic of the three I found very interesting was their senses of humor. Jack Plumley was a good time because he had more funny stories to tell than any other yarn spinner I ever met. As in the case of the Irving Trust guys, particularly Jim Ganley, this trait of Jack was very appealing, interesting and instantly friendly. I always knew that if I got a prospect in front of Jack, he would be of great help in landing the deal. Ray Meier looks like a boring professor. He is one funny guy off camera. He does imitations of people and characters that could put him on TV. He also loves a good time of a couple of drinks and spirited discussion over a wide range of topics. He's very smart. Boehlert, I found devoid of humor, always guarded and obsessed with politics. He seemed interested in nothing else. Perhaps it was me, but we never interacted as I did with the others. No laughs or letting one's hair down with Sherry. I have always found it interesting that in front of the camera he seems more personable than Jack or Ray but in reality he is less.

Being part of the Republican hierarchy and taking into account both party loyalty and their own ambitions, none were major innovators or visionaries. They were simply not prepared or willing to step out of the box in certain ways that might have prepared the county for needed future change. The political system from which they sprung did not foster nor encourage radical change. It was much easier to be "part of."

The stepping stone nature of the job and the goal of preserving Republican continuity trumped most other concerns. One fact strikingly illustrates this point. All three surrendered their jobs to give their Republican successors a leg up on elections. Oneida County has had nine county executives; five have been appointed, several of which were as acting county executive. There has undeniably been a system of using the job as part of a checker-board process under which Republicans hop from job to job, level to level. This has been good for them and the party but harmful to the area. The harm is that playing the game has stifled creativity and change. The system has bred loyalty to political party and position at the expense of the region. All of the county executives I worked with have played this political game and have contributed to the lack of governmental creativity and change that has plagued the area.

It is true, as stated by Jack Plumley, that there is not all that much real work attached to the executive's job. That could and should be seen as a plus, not a minus. A county executive is free to create ideas, to use the bully pulpit for change, to become an area ambassador for business development, to sell structural changes such as term limits and a host of more radical approaches and ideas. I found every county executive I worked with interested in and motivated by economic development. It is unfortunate that that level of interest and action did not appear in the nuts and bolts of overseeing and directing county government. Perhaps the realities of politics and the sheer depression of riding the elevator in the county office building are defeating. I have long felt that a county executive, who would limit his or her tenure to one term, and that one elected position, would be free to introduce and accomplish needed, overdue change. This more citizen oriented approach to the job may prove to be the path to elevating both county government and the politics of the entire area.

Business Development Change

The Oneida County Industrial Development Corporation no longer exists. It was merged with a group that had been formed to redevelop Griffiss after the flying missions left. However, the decision to merge development organizations and to locate the new entity at the Griffiss site was a harmful one. Both assuming the job of trying to redevelop an area as huge as Griffiss and locating staff and headquarters there wound up wrecking the balance of the Rome and Utica interests so carefully developed prior to the Griffiss loss. Trust, particularly from the Utica end of the county, was lost and the area quit working as a unified team on development projects. The sense that everything was going to Rome poisoned the well of development in the rest of the county. In many instances existing businesses and activities were checker boarded from one section of the county into Griffiss and existing business parks including our old park neglected. This may be the primary reason why no significant new development has been achieved since the mid-1990s. The Oneida County political leadership allowed the change and bears the responsibility for it.

Most seriously, the thought that what amounted to be a "new city" at Griffiss could be developed as Utica, Rome and the area were entering an era of decline, particularly in population, was foolhardy. The bite of the apple taken was much too big. There was no possible way that new development and new jobs could dominate and lead the redevelopment plan. There were simply too many thousands of acres and hundreds of thousands of building square feet to fill. And, a huge air field was accepted at a time the area had a smaller one with no commercial air carrier and little prospect to ever have one again.

The only possible result was to redevelop by checker boarding existing uses from other parts of the area into the former base. Tax breaks, loans, grants and below market lease rates have been used as enticements. This strategy simply takes for one part and moves to another. Net new jobs relative to massive public investment are extremely low in number.

As with the old urban renewal program, federal and state dollars thrown at closed military bases enticed areas, including our own, to make poor development decisions. Most important, the money stifled creative strategies and thought that might have resulted in a much more sensible, advanced and less costly redevelopment effort.

Lessons of the past were not learned.

Chapter Four

A Simple Twist of Fate: The Return to Utica— 2007

My sojourn into the private sector turned out to be quite a trip. As an executive with Dominic Chang's company, Family Golf Centers, Inc., I worked what felt like endless hours, traveled over 85,000 car miles a year, and made—and lost—a lot of money. I was in charge of developing our fifth facility in 1995. By 2000, we were a publically traded company of 158 facilities in 39 states. I was the Northeast Regional Director overseeing the development and management of 11 facilities in three states. The company was typical of the boom-boom 1990s and of that decade's stock market bubble. Our stock rose to an astronomical height for a company in our business and crashed with equal speed when our numbers failed to meet Wall Street expectations. But, it was one hell of a ride in between. If I had only completely cashed out at $42 per share! Hindsight makes it a lot easier to figure out. Greed plays a larger role in any kind of decision involving money than we'd like to admit.

One of the lessons I learned on the road with FGCI that's germane to this book related to local government and to my home area. As I traveled to carry out projects in other areas of upstate New York and into Massachusetts and Connecticut, I saw how different local governments functioned. Part of my job was to represent the company to the key elected officials of the areas in which we wanted to build and at hearings to secure the right to build. I quickly noticed two things. First, elected officials, particularly at city and town levels were much smarter and advanced than those in my home area. Second, much greater numbers of residents showed up at public hearings and other types of meetings. The democratic process was healthier. The fact that these other areas were larger and more prosperous was not lost on me. They were not as parochial and politically inbred. Even places like Clay and Henrietta, in the Syracuse and Rochester areas, seemed like separate worlds to Utica and Rome. Shelton, Connecticut was a difference of planets! This more enlightened and intense involvement by both elected representatives and the people they represented opened my eyes to the relationship between civic responsibility and progress in a very direct way. There is one New York story that touches on this point somewhat indirectly and was another eye opener to me.

An issue that hit close to home resulted from of one of my site/location inquiries on behalf of the company. A friend of mine from Rome who was a real estate executive called and asked if I'd look at a golf course complex for sale in the Glens Falls area. Before agreeing to the trip, I called Dominic to discuss whether or not we wanted to consider owning a full golf course in addition to range type practice facilities. He gave me the green light to look.

I met my friend at the Highland Golf Club located between Glens Falls and Lake George. My heart raced as I drove into the place. It was gorgeous! And, huge. The course was beautiful and the club house lavish. I learned that the property included over 100 acres of land for other types of development, including housing and a hotel, all part of a pre-approved master plan. The property was in bankruptcy because the local developer had spent more than he should have on the club house. The course and food business just couldn't support the debt secured through bank loans. The bank foreclosed and had the place up for sale.

My first thought walking into one of the most beautiful golf clubhouses I had seen was "casino." At the time, the State Legislature was considering designating four areas in New York as casino eligible. The Lake George/Saratoga area was one. And, part of the area was the home base of the high powered legislator Joe Bruno. He ultimately became Senate Majority Leader and with that, the most powerful Republican in the legislature. I never got to personally know him but I did observe him up close and often wondered how he reached the heights he did. He did not appear all that impressive. I surely thought that when the casino legislation was passed, the Bruno represented area would receive a designation. The idea of us owning, or flipping for great profit, a facility ideal for a casino development was irresistible. To understand the complete issue some background is necessary.

The Oneida Indian tribe had opened, with the Governor's approval, a casino in Vernon, NY in the mid 1990s. The ongoing legislative initiative was designed to spread the gaming wealth and development opportunities across the state. In other words, not to limit gaming to what amounted to a monopoly given to the Oneidas.

I called Dominic and urged him to immediately meet me at the Highland to take a look. He drove up from our Long Island headquarters the next day. He quickly agreed that the place was a knock out and that if bought at the right price, it could even make a go as a golf resort. He agreed that the casino possibility could create a very valuable upside. I told him not to worry because the state will not be stupid enough to leave a gaming monopoly in one place in the state. They turned out to be that stupid. The legislation did not pass. The Highland never became a casino, Vernon did remain a monopoly and the whole issue of Indian land rights has come to plague Oneida County for decades. Because we bought the Highland cheaply and eventually sold off the excess land for housing and other developments, we did not lose money. But, we sure did not make the fortune I envisioned. The hard work, the challenge and all of the large rewards with Family Golf later came to a screeching and sudden halt when its stock fell as the stock market bubble of the 1990s started to burst.

The financial condition of the company combined with back problems I had due to all the hours spent in a car traveling from location to location led to my resignation from the company. It was time to get off the road both literally and figuratively.

The Return

After taking a vacation, I started a self owned consulting firm that would include some activities associated with the Family Golf business and ties and an effort to drum up some local business development contracts. I was nervous about starting a new career at a relatively older age. I also was not sure I wanted to remain living in the Utica area. But, at that point, a move was not prudent.

In short time, I became affiliated with a small high tech type company that had been recently formed. The company's plan was to complete product development and to attract investment capital. The idea and potential of bringing a start up to market was interesting and challenging to say the least. One of the founders was a bit older than I and we shared an interest in developing a business that could both enrich us and help our home area. We partnered with some young high tech geniuses from Rome Labs who in their off time had developed some innovative product ideas relating to cell phone technology and usage. We concluded that we could form an effective group with the old men providing the business and finance sense and the young techies the technical expertise. The opportunity and interest was irresistible. So, we got to work.

Along the way, several twists occurred, including my brief plunge into politics and a very serious bout with kidney cancer. The cancer part sure hits home the message of life's fragility and was one of the driving forces behind the decision to write this book. The old "get it done before it's too late," kind of thing entered my thought process and I started to think about recording my slice of local history and experiences.

For a period in 2006, our business was slow and financing up in the air. We were working on an arrangement for investment that would take months to achieve. In the meantime, tasks and money were limited. One evening early that fall, I received a call from Tim Julian, the then mayor of Utica. He wondered if I wanted to meet with him to discuss coming to work for him. I agreed. There is a bit of background necessary to understand his call and my reaction to it.

Tim Julian is the brother of Bob Julian who is mentioned earlier in this book. I knew Bob much better than Tim. When Tim entered a Republican primary to run against the Oneida County Executive Joe Griffo for a State Senate seat, my wife and I offered to help. Tim was rebelling against the local Republican establishment which fit our style. We had been a part of a group waging the same type of battle in several ways since early 2000. My foray into politics mentioned involved challenging the Republican establishment by running unsuccessfully in a primary for Oneida County Executive against Joe Griffo. Tim seemed like a bright, feisty young adult who was not a career politician and who fit the rebel mold. He also had a good dose of street sense in his makeup. I liked that a lot. He seemed the type to shake up the Republican establishment which was long overdue on both the state and local level. Part of that shake-up ambition resulted from a view, that both Bob Julian and Tim held that their city was being treated unfairly by other levels of government most of which were Republican controlled. That pro city stance was compelling to this native Utican.

Bob, when he was a county politician, was a fierce defender of the city and believed that the city historically did not receive equitable treatment from Rome and suburban interests. I think both brothers recognized that Utica had become the dumping ground for the area's problems. By this, I mean that most of the problem population and social service type institutions supposedly created to help solve them were centered in Utica. The key point to grasp was that the Julian disenchantment with their own party was triggered by their perceptions of Utica's needs and inadequate political responses to them.

The backdrop to the Republican politics of the period is telling and continues to reverberate in the present. Griffo inherited his job as county executive by a political musical chair game conducted by Bob Julian, assisted by Ray Meier and then Governor George Pataki. In 2003, they moved to shift the sitting County Executive, Ralph Eannace, to a judgeship and replace him with Griffo. They feared Eannace could lose the Republican primary to me and that that would hurt the party. Part of the fear of Bob Julian was that Tim's run in the Utica mayoral race would be negatively impacted by this dissention in the ranks. I was viewed as an obstacle in the sense that I was both splitting the party and was not a team player, an assessment relayed directly to me by state senator Ray Meier.

In less than two years, the Julians, Bob and Utica mayor Tim, became challengers to the party status quo. They fractured from their own allies. The arena of challenge was the newly opened State Senate seat vacated by Meier who was running for the open congressional spot vacated by the retiring Sherry Boehlert. So, in a short period of time, several worms had turned. And, they were all trying to eat each other alive. Some team.

The reader will notice many of the same political names keep reappearing. This is indicative of the area which keeps recycling the same politicians from office to office, job to job.

This characteristic was adopted and championed by Governor George Pataki. I would argue that the downturn of the Republican

Party in the state and, in some instances, in Oneida County can, to a large extent, can be attributed to Pataki and his record. Pataki's post first term change from a fiscal conservative to a free spending liberal, near fanatic go-green proponent, turned a potential for growth to state wide economic decline. The Pataki-Bruno-Meier team produced little to nothing of substance for our area and probably contributed to the eventual political loss of Ray Meier himself. In his bid for Congress, Meir lost to a Democrat, the first Republican to ever lose in our congressional district. Yes, he did lose in the Republican slaughter of 2006, but Ray may have been better off if he had not been such a team player. An image of more independence may have served him well and his talents better suited to DC than to Albany. But, that train has left the station, for better or worse.

While on the topic of governors, I suppose I ought to mention my impressions of a couple more. Hugh Carey, a Democrat, was to me the best Governor of New York I knew and professionally experienced. Despite his party affiliation, he made his mark cutting personal and business taxes and constructing a very successful state development arm that among other things helped create Battery Park, the South Street Seaport and the Carrier Dome. I met him through Dick Assaro. As mentioned in an earlier section, Dick was an early Carey supporter and went to work for him. Carey was a good time, blunt, but very nice Irish politician throw-back, who was a gentleman first, politician second. He was entertaining and fun to be around. He also helped give rise to his eventual successor, Mario Cuomo.

In 1975, Carey named Cuomo his Secretary of State. Soon, thereafter, my then boss, Bill Valentine, learned that Cuomo was going to visit Rome to see our downtown renewal project. Valentine asked me to show him around after a brief meeting in the Mayor's office. Just the two of us then took a walk around the downtown. We talked baseball most of the time. Cuomo was a ball player at St. Johns and nearly made the big show. I pitched in my day and had a shot with the Pittsburgh Pirates. Neither of us made it but we loved the game. Cuomo seemed like a nice guy. Fast forward to him again being in Rome after he had been Governor for awhile. As the then IDC head, I sat in on a meeting with him. He had turned into a boring, pompous, thin-skinned, lecturer type. I liked the ball player a lot better. Enough of Albany; let's go back to Utica.

My wife and I had assisted in Tim Julian's state election bid in a few ways, but his call was still a surprise. I had come to like his moxie and dedication to the city in which I was born and raised. I thought he did have the independence to be a good state legislator while Griffo was sure to be a complete Republican insider. Julian lost the primary. He seemed shocked. Losing to Griffo has a way of doing that to people. He never seems like much but finds a way to win.

Part of me was fascinated with the idea of returning to Utica City Hall some 40 years after I left it. I was extremely interested on the comparison of times and the city. By then I had also already started the thought and shaping of this book. We met and I agreed to become Julian's Chief of Staff. That was the new name for the position of Executive Assistant to the Mayor which I held under Dick Assaro. I got a kick out of the upgraded importance of the sound of chief of staff. That has become kind of common, along with the mayor's wife being called the "first lady." The designation seems silly at a local level and was never used in the old days. I think it says something about inflated egos and expanded government. Although we had discussed other jobs, that job seemed best since I still needed to devote time to my company and I might only be able to work in City Hall for a relatively brief period of time. So, becoming a department head made no sense. I told Julian that when expected funding came through for the business, I would have to return to the company full time. We also determined that I could work on a few important matters such as helping to prepare the city budget and one or two industrial development projects that were stalled. Both were important matters since he was up for mayoral reelection in the fall of 2007.

I recall my first day on the job. As I drove into the City Hall garage, got on the elevator and entered my new office, I was struck by how little things had changed physically. It still could have been 1967. The building was in a time warp. As I left the elevator on the second floor, I noticed that the place was deserted. No one was there early. That was to be a harbinger of things to come. I settled into my office and to do what I could to help, my new mayor. My office was located almost exactly where I sat some 40 years before!

One of the mayor's development initiatives was a project with a company named Pacemaker Steel. The company is Utica based owned by F. Eugene Romano, one of the area's most successful businessmen. The proposed project was a relatively small one. It involved relocating the company from its old building in one section of the city into a new building in another. It was predicated on the goal keeping the company in the city and the creation of new jobs. Although the new jobs projected were relatively small, the mayor had embraced the project with strong support. I wondered why the project seemed to be stalled. I soon found out.

I met with the city's development director with the idea of offering him my help in any way he might need. As I entered his office, I noticed the IDA counsel was joining us. As we discussed the project, it did not take them long to come right out and state that they were against it. They did not think it merited the government money and effort involved. I recall asking them if they understood that the mayor, the guy they worked for, the chief executive of the city, wanted the deal done. They said yes but they would hope that I'd help talk him out of it. I was stunned and angry. The very idea that two of Julian's top guys were fighting something he wanted done blew my mind. I informed Julian of the meeting. Strangely, he neither seemed surprised nor did he share my anger. This one meeting was indicative of patterns and attitudes I soon noticed throughout City Hall. The place was totally disjointed. There was no uniform or concerted effort to accomplish. There was no esprit de corps. But, the mayor seemed unfazed and unconcerned. I could not grasp why. It was as strange a government/political situation I had experienced in a long career in and around politicians.

As pointed out in previous sections of this book, the mayors I had worked for, Assaro and Valentine, both generated and demanded loyalty. Yes, they encouraged internal debate but once they decided, it was decided, end of debate. They both had gentle ways of straightening out those who strayed and also had tougher keys guys around them. A Fred Nassar, a Dick Fahy and a Rodger Potocki could be pretty tough when pushed. There was no such loyalty or policy in Tim Julian's City Hall. It was the key reason why projects were not getting done and significant chunks of time and money wasted. Various arms of the city worked for well over a year on the Romano project and others. Consultants and their high costs were included. The very people, who were being paid to lead projects, were delaying, and eventually killing them. I had some thoughts about what might explain what was going on.

In selecting staff as he became mayor, Julian employed and rewarded holdovers, staff that was already in place. Part of the reason for that was the circumstance under which Julian became mayor in the first place. He inherited the job when the then mayor Ed Hanna, resigned amid scandal. Weird sex related charges involving Hanna and young men forced him out. Ed Hanna requires an entire book and even that may not be enough. I had known him since I was a little boy and my father knew him well. In short, Hanna was the most unhinged, controversial and outrageously behaving leader in the history of Utica; maybe in all of the country. Yet, to many he was god like. He had been elected mayor in two different intervals, at two times in his life. His last stint, when elected as an old man, Tim Julian was his running mate. As president of the common council, Julian became mayor when Hanna was forced out.

In becoming mayor under sudden and unanticipated circumstances, Julian retained the Hanna administrative team. I also would wager that Hanna had secured commitments from Tim on behalf of certain people and jobs as part of his resignation deal. This was to bite Julian in several ways administratively and politically. The holdover's loyalty to him was by and large thin and weak. In some cases, it was nonexistent. I came to believe that many were actually working against the mayor and his interests.

I also quickly learned that Julian had a tendency to make on the spot, impulsive decisions. He seemed to take pleasure in it. I even believe he hired me without thinking it through clearly or determining what he really wanted from me. In most situations hasty decision making is dangerous; politically, it is often fatal. Julian's hasty personnel decisions were a big problem. His snap judgments resulted in keeping some too long and hiring and promoting others too quickly.

In no time, I found many of the City Hall staff to be incompetent, lazy and disloyal. There was no drive, no zeal and very little ability with the exception of the mayor's office itself. There was always an excuse why something could not be done. The law office was a good example. The office was headed by a lawyer who had worked for previous mayors. She was a long-timer. Her work habits were questionable, her attitude to the mayor worse. They simply did not get along, at all. There was constant tension and infighting. The reader will recall how the importance I placed on city lawyers in the Assaro and Valentine days. Corporation Counsels were outside, smart attorneys who found ways for mayors to get things done. Julian's Corporation Counsel found ways to hinder. She disliked the Mayor and he her. Julian was always seeking ways to fire her. He never did. By the time I had arrived on the scene it might have been too late given it was an election year. In that year, her own brother gave Julian a Republican primary! That in-your-face insult may be the first of its kind in Utica politics. It reinforced his big mistake not to have inserted his own city attorney sooner. There were other very strange political goings on with other people Julian hired. One other publically considered running for mayor as he was taking a pay check from Julian! Other deficiencies of important departments were not as politically outrageous but represented serious administrative deficiencies.

The City Engineer's office was directed by a man who was not an engineer, nor did he seem to have much assertiveness in his own department. At one point I sat in on a meeting negotiating the upcoming CSEA labor contract. In the middle of the meeting, an extremely loud mouth union rep who worked in the engineering office started ripping the mayor in very stark, political ways. I objected and the meeting ended in rancor. The mayor and the engineering head were made aware of what happened and did nothing. In past days, she would have been immediately fired and consequences worried about later. The rules of the game had changed and not for the better. A department that functions from the bottom up and is dominated by union rules promoted by employees working against the mayor can cripple that mayor. This was the basic character of the engineering department as I viewed and experienced it. It moved at its own pace and with its own priorities. This was in stark contrast to the department I knew back in the Assaro days when Lou Critelli and Jim Kennedy were integral parts of the mayor's team both administratively and politically. Their counsel to Dick went beyond their job duty descriptions. And, performance was based on loyalty to both Dick and the city.

Utica's Urban Development department might have better been called the "no development" department. It was led by a director who, on paper, had no resume or deep experience for the job but had somehow secured a long term employment contract from Julian. I heard that he was a Hanna relative. This could have been one of those jobs Hanna protected when he left. Julian himself told me that his decision to keep and even promote this staffer was made in haste. Other than his planner, the rest of the development staff was weak and unproductive. Hundreds of thousands of federal dollars were thrown to this effort with virtually no meaningful results. Plus the staff constantly disrespected their own director. They had recognized as did I that he was not a leader. There is one relatively small but telling example of a so called development effort that illustrates the Julian staff problem and that of government itself. It involves a small public parking garage project.

The project was first announced in 2004. When I came in several years later, it was still on the drawing board. It became clear that the development department had no real clue to getting the garage built quickly and efficiently. The course taken on the project involved entering the morass of federal and state red tape tied to grant funding that wrecked any semblance of a well timed schedule. The locals seemed to have no idea of how to push the right bureaucratic and political buttons to overcome the inbred delays. Even in the red tape days of urban renewal, two larger parking garages were built in Rome quicker than the Utica proposed garage. As of this writing, no shovel of dirt has yet been turned. This and the failure to carry out the Pacemaker project efficiently are but two examples of the lack of development expertise and commitment that plagued the Julian administration at this time. In addition to slowing the City's progress, what resulted was Julian not being able to trumpet new development in an election year. Rufie Elefante's cardinal political dictum was to build at least one new building for every election cycle. Julian did not have one to showcase in 2007.

On the plus side, Julian was served by a competent and loyal office staff and accomplished leaders in the key areas of public safety. His secretaries, both Tim's hires, and a young man named Lou Parrotta, who worked as a part time publicist and advisor, were extremely loyal, productive and effective. I found the differences between the inside of the mayor's office to those located just down the hall striking and somewhat incomprehensible. Perhaps the situation was indicative of the mayor's different personalities. He seemed to be able to relax and stay focused with those in his office but high strung and unfocused with others. There were days of wondering which Tim Julian would show up. In the most important area of the government, the situation was different. They were the public safety functions, which were based outside of City Hall.

One would be hard pressed to find better professionals than the police and fire chiefs, Al Pylman and Russ Brooks. Both were loyal to the city and to the mayor. And, both gave good counsel to me the short time I was there. One of Brooks' officers was also running the Codes Enforcement Department. Interestingly, he was very productive and close to the mayor. This brought Brooks into our office more frequently. One of the more interesting ideas that developed was one of improving and intensifying the codes enforcement effort.

I had quickly and deeply become involved in codes for two reasons. A huge number of complaints being called into the mayor's office on a daily basis were codes related. One of my jobs was to answer the calls by making sure codes reacted to them. My talks with the department head, Frank Suppa were daily. I also believed that effective codes enforcement was one of the most critical tools in fighting the decline of residential life in Utica. That led to what I thought was an attractive and effective reform that would benefit the city and Julian's reelection.

That idea was to consolidate the codes enforcement activity into the Fire Department. I felt that would bring added professionalism to the department and get it out of the politics of City Hall. Suppa liked it, Brooks liked it and the budget director liked it. Julian approved further study. That was done, including discussions with cities like Albany which had consolidated the functions. We concluded that it should take place and that Julian should advance the plan as part of his reelection campaign. Julian's decision was to wait until after the election. As many incumbents erroneously do, he did not want to shake the boat prior to the vote. Most learn that postponing positive actions is not a wise political course. They learn it the hard way. In another irony, the concept of consolidation has recently been adopted by the city. Post Julian. The head of the other branch of public safety shared Julian's conservative nature.

Pylman was in City Hall on a regular basis reporting directly to the mayor. In the process of his doing that, he developed a habit of stopping in to see me and to discuss his department and its demands and problems. He was a very professional person who seemed out of place in the Utica setting. I don't think he was comfortable with the drug type problems of the streets, nor with the historical Italian American influence within the department. But, even though he seemed uptight, he conducted himself very professionally. He, however, resisted any and all ideas of new initiatives particularly those of a public relations nature. My sense was that he felt that they might imply something negative about his performance. There was another huge issue that impacted both Julian and Pylman that will be discussed later.

Julian's public works operation was headed by a guy, Bill Shraeder, who was hard working, highly professional and loyal to Julian. Julian himself loved to travel the streets and communicate needs to the department. I was very surprised to find a city DPW much better than I had experienced in the past. Sadly, the conditions in which they operated were much worse. Many Uticans simply did not seem to care about how their city looked. Trash and garbage were commonly thrown onto streets. I would personally witness this every morning on my way to work. Sidewalks weren't shoveled even on the downtown business district. It was constantly difficult for the DPW to keep up with the neglect of the very people it was trying to serve.

The differences between those department heads located outside of City Hall and those within were striking. I haven't answered why this was the case, but I do suspect that the basic reason has to do with a fact I pointed out earlier, that many were not Julian appointments in the first place. And, many were simply unprofessional. The buck stops at the mayor's desk when it comes to both keeping and hiring department heads since he controls those jobs. Lesser positions are more complicated. In that sense, Julian was not kind to himself.

The most glaring difference between the city employees of the past and those I saw upon my return to the building some 40 years later can be found in the word, zeal. In the late 1960s one walking into the building got the immediate impression those staffing offices were busy, happy and proud to be there. Most worked many extra hours for the pure joy of it. In 2007, the rush to the elevator at quitting time and the rushing in late in the morning told the tale. There was little spirit and virtually no zeal. And, there was not much fun or joy in the building. Most employees seemed to be disconnected and distant from the heart of the operation, the mayor's office. There was no spirit of people enjoying working together for a common purpose. I sensed a real difference in how public service employment had evolved.

The public employee question and the changes I noticed raise some questions that go beyond Utica and politics. Our governments, right down to the local level have, in my opinion, over institutionalized public employment. The expansion of unionism and its regulations and protections has harmed public service in important ways. The idea of the unionization of public workers was noble. It was founded on the protection of skilled, dedicated workers from politics. It was a counter to political patronage and all that went with it. The pendulum has swung too far. The public employee has virtual lifetime job security with ever increasing benefits. It is as hard to fire a City Hall employee as it is to fire a teacher in a public school. Performance standards are non-existent and a mayor or department head can't do much about a bad or disloyal employee. Although it is good that politicians can't shake down employees as mentioned in my Water Board story early in the book, it is bad that employees cannot be held accountable for on the job performance or positions easily reduced to save taxpayer money.

Ordinarily a good office staff, plus well functioning public safety and public works operations would result in a long serving mayor. There were offsetting issues with Julian. Perhaps the most important one was his inability and refusal to work closely with, or to try to orchestrate, the Common Council. Any city that has a severe split or clash between the executive and legislative branches will not be one of progress. Programs and projects stall or collapse and city image suffers when the branches do not peacefully and productively co-exist. In the Assaro days the coexistence was more difficult to achieve given the short two year mayoral term. With the reform to a four year term it should be far easier to build a sound relationship between the branches. This was not the case in the City Hall of Tim Julian.

Julian's administration was in near isolation from the Common Council in many ways. The split was severe. He did interact at a decent level with a couple of Republican members but there was no administrative strategy relating to moving projects through the

Council. He did not reach out to Democratic members or to all in his own party. The Ed Hill story is telling.

In my high school days, Ed and I played basketball and baseball together. Our basketball team was one of the finest to ever play at that level in Utica and Ed was its most outstanding player. He was also an extremely nice guy and very popular.

High school life in the late 1950s, early 1960s was wonderful, if you were white. If you were black, you were subjected to a type of academic segregation. Most male blacks were directed into industrial arts. Its shorter term was shop. They did not enter college preparatory classes. Ed is black and was caught in this limiting trap. When he was ready to graduate and college scouts came looking, it was found that he did not have the academic standing to be college eligible. In short, he was screwed.

Then, there was not an option for a junior college or prep school or any other solution one may find today. So Ed along with other talented blacks could not take full advantage of their talents and aspirations. Today, Ed would have been a star athlete at a good college. In 1960, he had to go to work. He and those like him were not stupid people. They realized what had happened to them and were angry. Many carry that anger throughout life. I sympathize with them. To understand them, you have to understand what the system did to them through the discrimination of disregard.

Julian's neglect of Ed Hill was not all that different of his neglect of other councilmen but it took on a stronger tone given Ed's background and pride. Julian had a tendency to move without properly informing Common Council members. In several instances, Julian encouraged legislation in Hill's district without Ed's input or knowledge. This slighted Hill more deeply and the alienation between the two grew. It cost Julian a council vote and someone who might have helped promote more progress in the city on several levels. I'm sure Ed shares in some of the responsibility in not meeting Julian half way. I also consider not being able to bring the two together a failure of mine.

When I worked for the executive branch in Utica and Rome years earlier, the cardinal rule was to solicit support from a councilman for a project specific to his district before legislation was sent to the full Council. For reasons I did not understand, this rule did not govern in the Julian administration. That was doubly surprising given Brother Bob's long career as a legislator on the county level. If anything of importance to his district or city went on without his knowledge, there would have been hell to pay.

I did understand Julian's problems with the Democrats. Their leadership was represented by members with very low intellectual capabilities, combined with a couple of them harboring their own mayoral ambitions. They were the opposing party. This combination was toxic and hurt any cooperative potential during that election year even if Julian had reached out for more cooperation. The bridges that had to be built needed to be built in the off election years.

Julian and the City

I had a very tiny window into the world of Mayor Julian's Utica. I worked there for a scant eight months. I caught him at the end of a cycle of sorts. His more positive accomplishments preceded me. Earlier, he had undertaken and realized some very important projects and changes. I also think that the city's performance in carrying out basic services was good to excellent under Julian. The downtown Utica Mutual project, his keen sense to leave public safety to professionals and his interjecting fight and spirit into the city was all admirable. I quickly looked into what I had identified as the most important measure of the administration, the population decline. I learned that for all practical purposes, the rate of decline which was extremely high pre Julian was pretty much halted during Julian's tenure. Prior to my leaving, I urged him to make this the centerpiece of his reelection bid. I suggested that he could sell himself as achieving the major accomplishment of halting population loss as the key prerequisite for leading growth. In other words, first stop the bleeding, and then heal the wound. But, as I observed his campaign from afar, he did not adopt that or any other theme. He simply ran on the fact that he was there as mayor and that people got what they saw. He did not try to sell himself in a coherent package related to the future of the city. He was a candidate running on a pat hand at a time when change was in the air. I translated his election staleness to my conclusion that deep down, as with Dick Assaro in 1971, he did not want to win. His bid for state office was both an indication that he wanted out of the mayoralty and that his popularity was low. His vote in Utica during that primary was nothing to write home about. He was also subjected to a primary in the mayor's race. He won but not impressively. And as with Dick, I think he was emotionally spent. The electoral conclusion for both was the same as well; the better person for the job did not win.

My tenure also coincided with personal, family problems he was experiencing. Having gone through my own at his age, I understood how screwed up one can mentally get. That might have been a major reason why his interest and performance suffered. Family problems are by far the toughest, especially when young kids are involved, as was the case with Julian.

To this day, I believe that Tim Julian was worn out trying to balance too many problems and concerns. He gave me the impression that he was actually sick of his job. He was, as said earlier bright, very quick thinking and could be energetic to a fault. He also had an undeniable love for the city. I think both the job and personal distractions simply defeated him as they defeat many in our journey through life.

But, when all was said and done, what most likely defeated Julian at the polls were events that had little to do with him or his people. There was a shooting that resulted in the death of police officer Thomas Lindsey in April of Julian's last year. And right before the election, another major shooting incident occurred. The deep cultural and behavioral problems of the City were spinning out of control. Julian and Pylman did not seem able to halt the chaos taking place on the streets. The voters sensed an out of hand crime problem. The weekend before the vote this most recent shooting drove home the voter fear at the most critical time. When it happened, I emailed a friend who worked at City Hall speculating that Julian just lost! The crime issue really played into a larger one.

Most seriously Julian did not articulate a rationale for hope in the future. While serving him, I wrote memo after memo urging him to articulate a new message that looked forward not back. I offered numerous suggestions of how to position himself and his aspirations for the city. He used none of my suggestions and, instead ran as a status quo candidate. Since I was gone during the heat of the campaign and he never asked opinions of me about it, I can't really say what made him think he could win his way. In fact, one of my lengthy memos identified who could beat him and how. This was the guy who ultimately did win, David Roefaro.

One can't understand Tim Julian and Utica politics, his actions and his ultimate political demise without understanding the deep changes within the city itself. Utica has seriously declined between when I arrived in City Hall in 1967 and returned in 2007. Its population is half of what it was. It has gone from a then city of 100,000 to one of 50,000. As important as the numbers is the loss of the more affluent, more educated resident who either left with businesses that migrated out of the area or fled to the suburbs. And, of the remaining population, a good deal of it was characterized by low income, under employment, high unemployment and a host of social problems ranging from mental disease, criminal conduct, sexual deviancy and drug addiction. The city also hosts a large segment of the area's elderly. The housing stock in the city's core neighborhoods is in awful shape and decline was starting to get noticeable in the so-called better areas. In other words, the city had become a dumping ground for the population no one else wanted while the more educated and affluent had fled. Particularly hard hit was the city's core. Old, previously decent neighborhoods in Cornhill, West Utica and parts of East Utica were disasters. Being Mayor of Utica was a tough job 40years ago; it was a near impossible job in 2007.

A basic realization of Utica's social decline could be discovered by anyone who even spent a day in the Mayor's office both seeing people and answering phones. People with the worst problems of mental instability and standard living needs would walk in off the streets for various reasons. Even danger of some nut getting out of control was always present. I, myself, defused several situations on the brink of getting out of control. The phone calls were worse. The filthy language and irrational demands from callers, dominated by the spoiled senior citizen demands for instant, all encompassing service were both wearing and discouraging. It did not take long in the mayor's office to wind up with a warped view of democracy in action. When I was Dick Assaro's assistant, I concluded that about 10% of Utica's population was unhinged, irrational, disturbed or experiencing addictions of some sort. In 2007, I estimated that percentage to be in the 30% range. Utica had become a dumping ground for the troubled. The tendency of Uticans to tear their own down had also dramatically increased.

What happened to Julian and Al Pylman raised the question about what I call the meanness of Utica and perhaps the area. This "tenor of the town" is a theme that runs throughout the book. Our area is a rough place and tends to be a small minded one, particularly when it comes to politics. Hurting people seems to be a public sport. Both Julian and Pylman were subjected to unwarranted personal attacks and slander. In Julian's case, the slander also harmed others. I'm sure it affected others in Pylman's life as well. I'm not going to get into details since they don't merit rehash or repeat. I've been around the block as they say so I put stock in my own feel. Nothing was anything but professional in the Mayor's office. Even some of our most so-called outstanding citizens spread unwarranted rumors about Julian not fit to print. It sickened me to hear it. I can only imagine how it disheartened the Mayor and those close to him. The city council with a disgraceful assist from the Observer Dispatch conducted a sham investigation of Pylman that was politically milked for all it was worth and mysteriously disappeared after Julian lost. The reason for the investigation itself was never made very clear. I know the expression of the "heat in the kitchen," but in my brief stay in the mayor's office in 2007, I learned that Utica was still a place where the politics of personal destruction was not only alive and well, but thriving as never before.

The changes within Utica have by and large been negative, with only small doses of the positive. As the demographics of the city changed dramatically between when I started my working life and when I served Tim Julian, so have the issues. They are important to discuss.

Utica, the Issues

I was born and raised in Utica. My birthplace, 1007 Jay Street, still exists. One always has a soft spot for one's birthplace. But, it is difficult to envision a bright future for the city. The reason relates to the inability and unwillingness of those who count to recognize, discuss and resolve what I call the real issues confronting the city and its future. This deficiency is most clearly apparent in the non-governmental sectors of the city including the business community and the media.

The city has a weak business base to begin with. There are few companies located in the city compared to the past having either left for suburban or Rome locations or left the area. Business leaders generally do not reside in the city. I think you can count those who do on two hands. The Utica Chamber of Commerce is run by those who are not of Utica anymore. Working for Julian, I was struck with the differences between the 1968 Chamber and the 2007 one. Dick Assaro never made a big move of any kind without talking to Chamber leaders. All I noticed in the Julian days was Chamber involvement in events and presentations, not policy and programs. Business heads with operations in the city were looking for tax breaks and other concessions and not involved in advising Julian on matters going beyond their own interests. This is perhaps a negative off shot of the expansion of government through tax relief, grants and loans that characterizes today's government /business relationship that was not present to a very large extent in the 1960s. How can a businessman take a Mayor to task, objectively advise, cajole and the like and then turn around and ask for money in one form or another. Today's relationship is built on campaign contributions and return favors. This has had a significant impact on business's role in shaping and moving government decision and policy making. This even places more stress on outside forces like the news media.

Since there is no TV or radio media left that generates local government news or reporting, the lone critical news force that impacts the city is the newspaper of record. The

Observer Dispatch for years had been characterized in a few key ways. It seemed historically fixated with one issue, that of downtown development. Even though all other elements defining and affecting downtown changed, the *OD* viewed it through an unchanging prism. It seemed that to the *OD* not much mattered and not much else deserved comment and coverage. I had always assumed that that was due to the fact that the *OD*'s property is located in the downtown thus creating a property value self interest. Also, the long time Publisher, Donna Donavan grew her trade in Burlington Vermont, and erroneously thought Utica's downtown could mirror that of Burlington's. No matter that Burlington has a downtown lake and a major downtown university. Back in City Hall I also learned that part of the problem was that inexperienced reporters with little investigative assignment or capability covered the city beat. In the brief time I spent in City Hall, behind the closed door, I marveled at the inability of an *OD* reporter to even ask a right question, let alone create an investigative path. I did notice, however, that as some different people started to rise in the paper, things did start to improve. An editor named Mike Kilian did take special note of an interest in the codes enforcement situation. A telling fact is that Kilian lived in the city, contrary to other *OD* big shots. And, today the paper, with even more new people, seems to be much more active in addressing some real problems. But, it continues to miss the big one, money.

The central, undeniable fact is that Utica is a bankrupt city. It cannot financially sustain the basic services it must provide.

The city's dilemma on the expense side is found in the cost associated with its two most important functions, police and fire. Both departments are unionized and both carry very hefty personnel salary and benefit costs. And, these costs escalated every year along with the rest of the employee union jobs in the city. When one factors in fringe benefits and built in escalating union contracts that govern most city workers, one recognizes the financial impossibility of the situation. Labor costs must be reduced in all ways involving reductions in personnel and in fringe benefits.

Utica is a classic case of an entity with declining revenue and increasing expenses. Over the past many years it has been staying above water by living on borrowed money and borrowed time. The financial reserves resulting from actions such as the sale of the municipal water system are nearly depleted. These reserves have been the only means the city has had to limit tax increases to relatively low levels. And, even the levels of these increases have caused business and population flight. The roof is about to completely cave in.

The city is characterized by potentially valuable property in the hands of tax exempt nonprofits, government union contracts and benefits that soar in cost annually, an old population on fixed income and being the home of significant numbers of people requiring the full range of social services government provides in today's America. Those characteristics do not make for a bright future.

There are answers yet no one seems to be talking about them. While the politicians dwell on social events, mediocre development projects and programs, and cronyism, the people on an annual road race and the newspaper on more coffee shops and bars, the city is dying. No one person has the solutions but it's not all that hard to ask questions and formulate answers. Raising the proper issues within the proper context is the only way to generate change and improvement. No one in or out of government in Utica seems capable or interested in even discussing, let alone solving them.

Utica absorbs most of the region's social problems and their cost. Cost in that sense is one of broad definition. You don't see many non taxpaying non profits owning key properties in the suburbs, except in the senior citizen service sector. You don't see registered sex offenders flocking to New Hartford. Rescue centers are in Utica. Most drug houses and low income housing projects are in Utica. Yet, the region has, to a large extent failed to share in the direct and indirect cost of this condition. So, one cannot look at city fathers for complete blame and responsibility for the decline in the integrity of the city's identity, size and prosperity.

But, elected leaders do have the duty to formulate an approach of sacrifice, cost restraint and change of government structure that may help preserve the city. The same question can be asked of the school board and public unions. Can city priorities be rearranged to reflect more realism? For example, why not use hundreds of thousands of dollars of federal funds currently spent on unproductive programs like business visitations, tiny business loans for fluff like building facades and more bars and a host of baloney that just one city department wastes and pour that money into basic services? Swallow pride and recognize a bad project and foreclose on a hotel that does little for the city's fabric. Or, use political connections to have HUD write off the city's obligations. It can be done. Recruit a committee of academics to voluntarily study and recommend new sources of revenue. Commuter taxes and service fees the non profits should pay are but two examples. Decades have gone by as concepts like regional tax based sharing plans have even been raised let alone implemented. Perhaps this alone could lead to effective consolidation. These are but a few ideas. But, the real question is one of population.

The most important question of all is how to convince talented, industrious immigrants to remain in the city and to help lead its renewal. The area has already lost industrious, entrepreneurial driven immigrants to other more prosperous areas of the country. And, the urge for those who remain in the area to leave the city for suburban life will also continue. The city and its community leaders and institutions must create strategies that result in an environment that fosters immigrant investment and residential commitment to Utica. This is no easy task.

All resources in thought money and creativity ought to be devoted to increasing revenue, lowering fixed cost, stabilizing residential neighborhoods and upgrading schools. Downtowns, job creation and festivals are nice sounding from a political perspective but are insignificant to the real problems and needs of the city. What good does it do the city when people come into work, to dine, drink coffee or drink to only return to their home or apartment in New Hartford or Whitesboro where they pay taxes? Yes, some sales tax revenue is good but is small potatoes. Utica, as any city needs a stable, growing, taxpaying residential population base to survive as a viable urban center. That residential population and tax base is, and has been significantly declining over decades. People much smarter than I used the phrase; pave the streets, as a metaphor to describe basic service concentration. A drive on the streets of Utica tells the story. In most sections the streets and houses are in a sorry state of disrepair. This one simple observation says a lot about both the changes that have taken place in the city and the misplaced priorities of local government, the media and the population in general. Many residents in many sections have no pride in their property or city while the city fails to take steps to help engender that pride. Virtually all resources should be targeted to stabilizing residential neighborhood and life. Money and personnel should not be wasted on failed development concepts, unnecessary functions and political patronage. Strong neighbor-hoods and a stable, growing population are the only foundations that will save the city. And, they are the only investment that can spur the return of commercial growth. People produce commerce, commerce does not produce people.

There are neighborhood bright spots. Bosnian and Russian immigrants have bought and improved both residential and commercial neighborhood properties. The Rev. Maria Scates has performed a miracle in the middle of Cornhill. She credits God. Cassandra Harris-Lockwood has a training center concept that could provide invaluable trades training if fully implemented. Churches like Our lady of Lourdes in South Utica are alive with people and activities designed to promote stability. Public safety initiatives are gaining strength. How does Utica multiply the bright spots?

What is lacking is an overall grasp of not only the proper priorities but the urgency to reorder and to create innovative solutions. There is a crisis of leadership that includes but is not limited to City Hall. Political, business and media leadership must get out of the anachronistic box in which they have been living. The solution to this crisis of leadership is the one upon which the future of Utica waits.

The problems of the city started to develop long before Tim Julian became Mayor. The leadership vacuum within sectors like the business and media communities on top of the declining civic capabilities of city residents resulted in Julian's job being a very lonely one. Part of that loneliness was self created but most not. The city's leadership vacuum must be filled from outside of City Hall.

In 1965, *What Utica Needs*, raised the same question of leadership and advanced both the people and ideas to answer it. That movement failed for reasons already described in this book and for some that will be discussed in the final chapter. Utica, 40 years later, needs a new *What Utica Needs* and a new movement of new leaders and creative new ideas. The old Utica will never return. The sooner those who care for the city realize it, the better. This native of Utica often wonders if it is not too late for the city. One hopes and prays that it is not. For, if it is too late for Utica it may also be too late for the entire area.

Chapter Five

Lessons Learned

This book was written for three reasons: to record a slice of history, to provide some interesting insight into personalities and issues, and to help present and future generations understand the area's past as a tool for dealing with its future.

If one left the area in 1965 and returned today, one word, decline, would describe the change. As described in the book, there have been significant wins and losses in the area's struggle to grow and to maintain a vibrant community. But, overall the area has been losing that struggle. Tens of thousands of people have left taking their brain power and wealth with them. One can argue that all of upstate New York has experienced a similar modern history. That is true in one sense and not another. Yes, the upstate New York battle has overall been a losing one but the fact remains that most upstate communities have fared better than that of the Utica-Rome area. Our area is simply poorer, older and less educated than all other upstate urban areas. In terms of national demographic trends, we lag even more. What explains this condition?

Fate and politics have not been kind. Outside events beyond local control seriously impacted opportunities for dramatic, positive improvement. For example, if Bobby Kennedy lived and became President of the United States, the Kennedy-Assaro connection have likely would have had a dramatic impact on the area. Although some would have moved on to greater heights in state or national positions, the Utica area would have been on the map. Fred Nassar and many others would not have forgotten their home city. Could Griffiss Air Base been saved by a more effective political effort? Was Boehlert's inability to keep a seat on the Armed Services committee the beginning of the end to the Base? It is easy to say yes, but other bases in more powerful congressional districts were also closed or depleted. In our case, the failure to align ourselves with the Air Force with the photonics lab project was a serious blow to the Base's future. Even if flying missions were lost, there would have been even more technical missions and jobs to overcome the loss. Was there any circumstance under which the downtowns of either cities Utica or Rome could have fought off the onslaught of the suburban mall? Not many, anywhere, did. Our area, however, was smaller and more manageable than most. Sensible consolidation as advanced by several in the mid 1960s, if achieved, could have led to more sensible and efficient growth strategies and policies. There is no doubt that structural change would have lowered cost and taxes. It may have been enough to counter New York State taxation policies and may have even served as a model to both other areas and to the state. Our area had the potential to be the showcase for New York State.

Monday morning quarterbacking is fun and all too easy. It's much more instructive to deal with what we absolutely have learned and do know as fact. Poor political decisions severely harmed the area. Neither elected leaders, nor those who elected them, spurred governmental, structural, or tax policy that had a shot at affecting positive change that could have resulted in a modern government configuration molded to meet modern demands and trends. The area still to this day exists with centuries old political boundaries and institutions. The area's business community did not step forward to insist on necessary political change or to help create innovative solutions to business and educational development. The people's involvement and participation in key aspects of the civic life and responsibilities have spiraled downward. The important lessons to be learned that may help explain what has happened to the community can be grasped by looking at the community elements of the political, business, media and the citizen as observed over these years. An understanding of these lessons may bring insight into future adjustments and changes that just might contribute to advancing the area.

Political realism allows us to draw a few key conclusions. Political stars only rarely get aligned in unique ways that may result in dramatically altering a community. The stars were aligned uniquely in the mid 1960s. And this book described how this alignment all too quickly disappeared. Key leadership and key relationships were lost. The remaining period was characterized by rather normal, mediocre political players in competency, style, and character. Our political leadership bullpen and potential for achievement has gone from excellent and competent to barely making the grade. There is simply no comparison in competency and potential between the Utica under Assaro and the Utica under Julian. Valentine's Rome was more vibrant and compelling than what followed. Lanigan's Oneida County government talent has not since been matched.

As I've known and observed political actors close up, I have no doubt that the public arena is entered with noble intentions. There is also little doubt that the price one can pay to achieve political leadership, to maintain it and to grow it often runs counter to the altruism that spurred the ambition in the first place. Political power and all that comes with it is a powerful intoxicant. Keeping it becomes the mission of the office holder and those behind him.

One of my favorite movies is called Viva Zapata. I was surprised to learn that the movie is a favorite of John McCain, the 2008 Republican presidential nominee. In the movie, Marlon Brando plays the lead as the Mexican revolutionary Emilio Zapata. Zapata himself is a peasant who rises to lead the peasant inspired revolution depicted in the movie. Zapata gets his leadership start when he represents a group of peasants in front of the ruler of their province. He makes a radical request in blunt and challenging terms and the ruler turns to an aide and whispers, "Take down his name." The implication is that they will note, watch and perhaps bring harm to this troublemaker. Zapata, himself eventually wins power and sits in the same chair as the boss he deposed. As the situation in the countryside does not improve, a bunch of peasants come to meet Zapata to demand relief. One is blunt and challenging. Zapata turns to his aide and whispers, "Take down his name." He immediately realizes that he has become what he fought against. He bolts to return to the countryside. The lesson is that power corrupts. The Brando character bolted, but that is pretty much the fantasy of Hollywood. Political power is rarely surrendered. Most have to be carried out.

The reality is that the political instinct is to hold on to that power by doing whatever it takes to keep it. That instinct of the preservation of the political status quo has dominated the area throughout the period of this book. And, the longer the political status quo is maintained the more consuming it becomes. This becomes exhibited in both policy decisions and in the actual character and temperament of those holding office. The behind the scenes actors often are more power driven than those elected. This political instinct goes a long way in explaining the absence of enlightened, creative political leadership. It helps explain why the Assaro people were rushing to recruit and give jobs to those they recently defeated. The power of the Kennedy potential and what it offered was irresistible. It helps explain the hubris of Jim Donovan that lost the photonics lab, the weakness of Sherry Boehlert, whose primary goal was political self preservation. It likely explains Ray Meier not effectively pursuing the governmental consolidation he knew was vital to the area's future. The fear of the implications of more political power held Bill Valentine back. Jack Plumley understood it more than anyone, played the game while trying to reform but then fled when he got turned off by the very system he headed. These characteristics of local leaders as described in this book are not unique to our area. They are part of the democratic framework as it has evolved in

America from Washington, to Utica and Rome. This drive to hold onto political power has serious implications to the entire question of leadership in our society. In turn, it has had negative impact on our prosperity and growth.

In many areas, politics and political leadership is reactive rather than proactive. Basic services are provided. Some areas provide it better than others but performance is usually in a rather normal range. It is the, going beyond the basics that separates the average political leader from the excellent. Bill Valentine attempted to go beyond the basics when he bit off the job of trying to remake so much of Rome. In other cases both fate and personal decision making interceded to negatively affect the reach to excellence. Assaro lost Nassar, Kennedy got shot and a dream that could have been realized also died. Tenney and Cardamone chose the bench. Lanigan went to Albany and took talent with him He and they did not look back in any important way. These were the leaders who represented a potential of excellence that could have led the area to heights unreached. Their successors with whom I worked and knew well, were politicians concerned more with traditional, less daring and less creative insights, ambitions and dreams. Their performances were more limited by their own limitations associated with their view of the political. This does not make them bad or evil. And, most important, it is unfair and inaccurate to place the condition of the area at their feet of responsibility. They are but part of the tale.

The political arena does not by itself determine the future of any area. Politics and political personalities are fleeting. As we evolved from the boss controlled days to the modern, the nature of the political also changed. Communities required a much larger base of the civic brought on and required by modernity. New categories of leadership formed in many areas along with new responsibilities and goals. The Utica-Rome area did not make the modern transition as some other older and most new communities did. It remained over reliant on politics and government; on the old ways. Civic responsibility and participation did not evolve here as it did in many other areas. Many new players outside of politics drove governmental reform in these other areas. Private sector groups and institutions led change.

Here, the political landscape has existed within a government structure that promotes administrative frameworks, policies and programs that are relics of that past. The population of Oneida County is over 30,000 less than it was in 1967. Both central cities hold half the populations they did. Yet government agencies either remain the same in size and type or in some cases grown. Sparse public resources are spent on zoos, air ports and performing arts centers that cannot be supported by the existing, smaller population base. Almost every municipality retains a library and police force. Dreams of past bustling downtowns, as unrealistic as they are, exist and are promoted with public funds. Government positions, pension demands and other fringe benefits grow while the tax base shrinks. An observer from another planet would conclude that the area is on a suicide mission, one based on the unwillingness or inability to change.

In the mid 1960s, government expansion was on the rise, particularly in creating urban oriented programs. The Great Society was the cure all. Over the decades, government expansion has increased in most areas of American, New York and Utica-Rome life. And, it has largely failed us and our communities. Successful communities did not put all of their eggs in the government basket. The Utica-Rome area never quite looked far enough to other avenues of growth and change. As described in this book, I've witnessed and been a part of failed Urban Renewal, failed public housing, failed public welfare programs and failed government involvement in the business arena. Government has overreached and our local politicians of both major political parties bought into it as the area's key to growth. If only Albany or

Washington gave us more. That refrain is heard on our streets to this day. The government dollar was as irresistible to Tim Julian and Ray Meier as it was to Dick Assaro and Bill Valentine. The huge difference is that the activities and money that is needed to support them have grown significantly over the years. And, the greater the growth of government, the greater becomes the reliance on it. This characteristic of ever rising political and governmental dependency has brought great harm to the area and perhaps doom to its future. It has brought higher cost and greater inefficiencies. Most seriously it has weakened the core of civic responsibility so necessary to a vibrant community.

The forty year journey described in this book began with the idealism of a young public servant convinced that government and those who controlled it could create the good, prosperous, growing, enlightened community. It ended learning that government weakened and in some cases poisoned what it set out to cure. Perhaps this poisoning of the well of government and politics could have been altered or reversed if not for a striking fact.

That striking fact which is relatively unique to the Utica-Rome area is the lack of accountability of local political parties and elected officials that has been evident over the past couple of decades. When I worked in the City Halls of Utica and Rome, local government operated under a microscope. And, performance was demanded among all segments of the community. That has changed in recent years. The same parties, controlled by the same people, acting and governing the same way have been the norm. The political system has basically been left alone to run unchanged. How else can one explain the electoral success of those who have produced failure, not accomplishment? How else can one explain the one party rule of the county legislature for the 40 year period covered in this book? We must look deeper to understand how a political status quo exists in the face of overall area decline.

Areas that have grown prospered and adjusted to changing conditions have been those where other sectors of the community lead the politicians and governments in community decision making. They tell the political; they don't ask for from the political. In these areas, private money and investment has far outstripped government money and control. In every other area I have worked in and observed, the private sector has been far more active in civic affairs, direction and investment than the political sector. The modern Utica-Rome model is the opposite. The private sector grouping of the business community, the media and the average citizen have, in most ways allowed and followed, not insisted, and led the political. An overview of these groupings will help explain that condition.

The Business Community

The Utica-Rome area's business relationship with the political has significantly shifted over the years. Dick Assaro never decided anything important of public consequence without checking with the head of General Electric, the city's largest employer. Bill Valentine did not make a public move without consulting with a Bob Lake or Charley Getty of Revere Copper and Brass or with Buell Hinman of Rome Strip Steel. County government was a much smaller player in public affairs since the suburban explosion had not yet happened. As it did develop the business community assumed a more formal role in area wide development activities. One vehicle created was the Oneida County Industrial Development Corporation. The model established by this group was one of private sector control with some government support. This partnership model was based on the premise that the business community was best equipped to attract and generate more business and, therefore, more prosperity for the community. In other words its foundation was the private sector.

No one is so naive to assume that the motivations of the business community were completely noble. Many certainly had a vested interest in preserving the status quo of things like labor availability and cost. Some, I'm sure wanted to keep out as much as to attract in. But, my sense is that the positive far outweighed the negative.

When I worked for the organization, I never got any pressure not to bring in competing businesses. My board of directors had pretty hands off approach to the day to day activities of the organization. My executive committee, a small group which really ran things, was largely comprised of bankers and lawyers. Bankers and lawyers always want new business coming in to become new clients. Until this group got deluded a couple of years before I left, they were committed to the mission of attracting new industry even if it did compete with existing companies. But, the regional approach of the OCIDC model did not translate into the business community leading change in other sectors of community life.

On two occasions, county executives, first Boehlert and then Plumley, held summits largely geared toward and attended by business leaders that were designed to foster regional approaches and solutions to area problems. Special committees were formed to study and recommend reforms to such matters as taxation, consolidation of services and local government structure. I can't recall anything of substance that came out of any of these committees or studies. There was no follow through or insistence by the business leader geared to structural governmental change or in creating new, innovative approaches to common problems. For example, a concept called Tax Based Sharing was discussed and studied. This approach was designed to spread the wealth of taxation generated by new development. It was studied to death.

Over the past couple of decades, the business characteristics of the community radically changed. Many companies who were headquartered here either left or were bought up by outside companies. As a result, the local connections became less important and less emphasized. The cultures of businesses changed as well and less time was given to executives to become community involved. And, with the feeling that politics was somehow beneath the business station, many did not, and do not want to, get their hands dirty. When I was OCIDC head I had a specific contact high up the GE food chain who kept me informed of not only what was going on but on what the company expected. This contact, a terrific guy named Ed Peterson, played a key role in helping to realize the GE expansion into the Utica Business Park. When the local GE operation got to be part of the Martin Marietta banner, contacts and context changed.

Most important of all, the big business players of GE, Bendix and others have left the area all together. And, with them, they took away a middle management class vital to community growth and improvement.

My experience as related in this book leads me to one undeniable conclusion; the business community has evolved into a defender and promoter of the political and social status quo of the area. It has also been resistant to change and innovation in several critical ways. It has not significantly challenged the existing political order instead it chooses to work within it to extract benefits. Today's government of tax policies and regulations has led to business asking from government as opposed to demanding actions from government. Much of what is left of the business community has grown dependent on government and, therefore politics. There is a partnership to preserve rather than to change and grow. In the past, the politician dared not cross a powerful business leader. Today, many local business leaders dare not cross the politician.

The local business community has also been less than innovative as it helps manage business development activities through various development groups. Internal private business decisions are bottom line based in the sense that risk/reward and cost/benefit relationships are constantly analyzed and reviewed. This business sense and characteristic seems to desert business representatives when they oversee public or quasi-public programs and expenditures. The staffs of business development agencies in reality run the agendas and the performance. If these staff operatives are not sharp, not leading edge and not independent from political pressures, the results are mediocre at best; wasteful and counterproductive at worst. Business leaders are in place to see that this does not happen. They have by and large failed this charge. There are several understandable reasons why that are a raised in this book.

Time limitations, reliance on government money, political ties and absentee ownership are a few characteristics of the local business arena as it evolved over the years. Today's business also requires much more time than yesterday's. As competition became global, money tighter, government rules and regulations expanded, the business executive understandably has little time to spend on so-called community development efforts. Over a fifteen year period at the OCIDC, I saw my board leadership weaken insofar as oversight and involvement as years went on. For example, the old style bankers of Oneida National Bank and Marine Midland had a lot of time, deep roots in the community and egos that resulted in their being the boss in everything they were involved with. The modern banker of the consolidated, global financial sector has no such time or roots. And, as government has increased its financial involvement in private sector affairs, it is not generally subjected to the wrath or pressure of the business community. This lack of tension is not healthy. Finally, there simply are not as many home grown companies as there were. And, no matter how noble corporate HQ located out of the area may be, its attention and dedication to a particular community will not be anywhere near as strong as ownership living in that community.

issues. The in depth reporting present in the past is not there. The area's market is so small; the TV and radio stations devote little to public matters. When I started more than one radio station covered City Hall with a daily presence. Utica TV channels have never been characterized by in depth reporting or editorializing.

The Citizen

Ultimately, the worth and value of a community is measured through the people who live, vote, pay taxes, worship and work in that community. When the question is asked, "what happened here?" the cliché of looking in the mirror is applicable. The ability to fully describe the dynamics and characteristics of the people of the Utica-Rome area is beyond this one book and its author. Perhaps another book, or series of books, will be written to delve more deeply into the topic. As a lifelong observer of the area fortified with the experiences described in this book, I have drawn some impressions and conclusions.

A significant part of the population may be likened to the proverbial herd of sheep, wanting and waiting to be led. This can be best explained and understood by two phrases that hold deep meaning in understanding this part of our population. The first is, "A mill town with a mill town mentality," the second, "Crumbs Along the Mohawk."

My own roots are of the mill town. I was born not far from the mill my grandfather worked in sharing a house with aunt and uncle mill workers. My family was of Polish immigrant stock. Many of our neighbors were Italian immigrants. Our common characteristic was being poor and uneducated. Life in my neighborhood in Utica, NY at that time, the 1940's, was dominated by bosses. The authority figures of the mill owner and the foreman ran the workplace and controlled the paycheck that was needed weekly to feed the family. Every day life outside of the workplace was strongly attached to the church which required attention, devotion and abeyance. One did not cross the priests or nuns in any way. Politics and government were controlled by the boss, Rufus Elefante. And, there was always the specter of organized crime in the background. Life was simple and basic because it was highly structured and controlled. Rebels and free thinkers were few and far between. The concept of change was an anathema. Expectations were measured and limited. The expression of the mill town mentality is often misinterpreted to mean, dumb. It actually means subservient. This attitudinal feature of the working class became part of the community characteristic transferred from generation to generation.

I experienced this first hand in 1965 and 1967 when Italian-American families literally split over the Assaro to Elefante challenge. Sons and daughters who supported Assaro were in many cases thrown out of the household of their parents. Such was the attachment of an obligation to, "the Old Man". These characteristics in many ways exist in large segments of the older population demographic today. All too many look back, not ahead. This can be attributed to the surrendering of responsibility to govern one's own future and the future of one's community. The looking to others for power and direction, engrained in the Italian and Polish immigrant classes has continued. Many still look outside of themselves for verification. It is stunning to me that today's Utica politicians still frequently refer to Rufie. These politicians are the sons, daughters, or grand kids of those who grew up with the immigrant mentality. Many still cling to it as if it was inherited. They seem to cherish it. This trait has had profound implications to the lack of aspiration and drive to independence, self assuredness and the resulting excellence required to lead or contribute to advance ones community.

I think that was the basis for a very smart, clever cartoonist named Randall Kimberly to name his cartoon feature "Crumbs along the

Mohawk." In the early 1990s, a Kimberly cartoon was published weekly on the editorial page of the Sunday *Observer Dispatch*. It was a brilliant feature, both clever and telling. It was so telling and controversial that the cartoonist got fired. To me, Kimberly's title said that those along the Mohawk were satisfied with "crumbs." In other words, expectations and aspirations within the area were low. Therefore, the area would stay as it was and the people content with the status quo. To not expect more is to not achieve more. The relationship between the mill town mentality and crumbs is striking. It also ties into levels of education.

Recently, the area has significantly lagged behind national and state educational achievement levels. We have a population base not as smart as that of other areas. Low levels of education have an obvious relationship to aspiration and expectation. As our educational levels declined with population loss so have our aspirations. Our expectations remain low as does our self-image.

The immigrant class of my grandparents and the immigrant parents of those older than I, in fact instilled great aspiration and expectations in their young. People who barely spoke English, let alone school educated, understood the great hope and opportunity of America. As a young kid living in a poor, Polish sliver of East Utica, I recall the Sunday drives to look at the homes of the "rich" and being told that I could someday own one. We children were discouraged from speaking Polish so we could more quickly become, "American". We were to be doctors and lawyers. This immigrant characteristic of hope in and aspiration for the future served as the backdrop for political awakening.

The Assaro Movement, led by Nassar and Assaro, both products of the immigrant mentality, was based on the premise that the area had to break out of the old, the status quo and reach for the political moon. They grasped and embraced the idea of change and stuck their necks out to lead it. Fred Nassar loved the immigrant characteristics and values. He embraced them and lived them. At the same time, he knew that they had to be adapted to radical change if the area was to grow and prosper. As it turned out, that realization and what happened to the Assaro dream was the only time in the 40 year history of which I write when radical political change surfaced and succeeded to the point of capturing a high local political office, the mayoralty of Utica. Its failures ended the only serious lurch toward major change that occurred in the years covered by this book.

The next thirty some odd years were featured by establishment politics and political leaders who were interested and committed to maintaining it. Even those who were not a key part of the internal political order, like a Bill Valentine, did not challenge it. He, Boehlert, Plumley and Meier were all competent, honest and decent men. But, they were not game changers. They played within the rules and structures of their political party to a large extent and they did not rock the boat. Most important, they were not visionary in the sense of seeing a future that could not be sustained by the status quo.

That became strikingly and tragically clear in the years between 1995 and 2003. The area was hit by an economic tsunami. Griffiss Air Force Base was lost, Martin Marietta left as did Chicago Pneumatic, Bendix, Oneida Limited and a number of important smaller companies. Rome Labs was not lost but now employs half the people it did at its peak. The technical managerial class has been particularly hard hit. Along with these came the loss of population. Utica is half the size it was 40 years ago, Rome the same; since the mid 1990s the area has lost nearly 30,000 people. And, lost from the age and income demographics that no area could afford to lose. The most significant impact of this decline has been the drain of brainpower and the loss of talented creative young adults.

The loss of Griffiss Air Force Base was of particular importance in this writer's opinion. Not only did it result in a significant number of direct and indirect job losses but the loss of the military factor was equally significant. The Base brought people into the area from all parts of the country. This brought with it experiences and points of view that added to the collective knowledge, experience and flavor of the area. Many of the Air Force officer class were among the best and brightest residents. Significant numbers of them wound up choosing to retire in the area thus continuing their positive impact. The loss of the military missions on Base ended this human capital source that is difficult, if not impossible to replace. The Martin Marietta, formerly GE, loss was equally as devastating in both economic and human resource ways. These losses resulted in radical change to the socio-economic characteristics of the area in a very short period of time. The worst case scenario came true. An "old" community was left to deal with it.

Although the area has changed—it is smaller, less wealthy, and less capable in important ways such as maintaining its tax base— its governmental structure has remained the same. To get hit in the head with the knockout punches the area received but not to react creatively to them is seriously flawed. Amazingly, the status quo governmental structure remains. Unfortunately, there continues to be little recognition let alone action to change that status quo even as it becomes obvious that it is financially unsustainable. Public policy is not reacting to the need for reform nor is the population demanding it in large enough numbers. Important segments of the population simply continue to leave for greener pastures.

As the economic/political pie gets smaller, the more the political and social establishment seems intent on maintaining the status quo. But, as pointed out by history elsewhere and experienced that hard way here, communities do not remain the same; they grow or wilt, they move forward or drift backward.

My 40 plus years of recollections are a mixed bag of emotional, intellectual and personal memories worth recording. That is the basis for this book. But, its purpose goes much deeper. That purpose is to lend an understanding insight into where we've been as a way of helping today's community grasp where we have to go. Those who have pointed out failures, pointed out short comings and have urged change have often been branded as negative. But, that label is just a meaningless one designed by established interests to stifle serious discussion and debate within the community. The integration of life style, social and economic status quo by one segment of the population has fed right into the hesitancy to be aggressive and dynamic in the broader base. Demographically, we are one of the oldest areas in the entire country. That has obvious and profound implications for the future, none positive. Can this handicap be overcome? Can the younger blood that does remain or new blood immigrating in lead a transformation from decline to stability to growth?

The American Dream is based on the belief that the future will be better than the past. This basic premise inspired our immigrant forefathers, our parents and those of current generations who have worked hard to provide better lives for their families. That is what a community is all about. Whether or not the future of our slice of central New York will be better than our past is still an open question. Who will answer it and how?

My inside the room experience has dramatically changed my conclusions about government and how it operates. I entered public service during the 1960s when the service was viewed as both noble and of great potential to lead change, growth and the capture of, the better live for people. I was not unusual to feel that civic responsibility was best carried out from within politics and government. Forty some odd years later I would answer Jack Kennedy's quote of, "Ask not what your country can do for you," by concluding that civic leadership and responsibility is best carried out from outside government, and that government's role in a community ought to be limited to the basics. The principle that government should do less and do it better and more efficiently should be reinstituted in public affairs. Over the decades very few efforts beyond the basics have worked in the Utica-Rome area. The public arena can't force people where to shop, where to invest money, where to live or how to run their personal lives. We are simply wasting a lot of time and money on the same failed, shop worn attempts by the governments to shoe horn behavior into the old rather than acknowledging the new. Precious human and financial capital should not be drained on schemes, activities, subsidies, that serve little purpose but that of political headlines and ultimately fail.

If we reduce the size of our governments, its layers, numbers of people, and meddling, more of our money and attention can go into the civic institutions of church, new education options, issue oriented local think tanks and private sector job creation development. Political leadership as the linchpin of community progress and growth has not worked. Politics and politicians should follow, not lead. The future must be determined from below, not above. If the ordinary citizen does not pick up the mantle of civic responsibility, involvement, education and change, the area into which this author was born will slowly but surely disappear.

Tocqueville so eloquently made the observation that a nation of followers may not be capable of self government. In the Utica-Rome area, an area characterized by followers, decline has been the inevitable result. If that decline is to be reversed, the area must reach a new, dynamic level of civic involvement, understanding and commitment. A leadership of knowledge, courage, experimentation, resolve and plain guts must emerge from within all sectors, private and public. Boldness and sweeping change are required. If a level of leadership exhibiting these characteristics does not emerge in quick order, the area will never recapture its past prosperity and optimism.

Postscript
The Future

In discussing this book with others, I've been asked if it would address future needs. My initial reaction to the question was, no. A book of recollections designed to both help fill in the historical record and interest the reader is by nature a book that looks back. And, the book only deals with issues, people and events in which I had direct involvement. But, as I kept thinking, I changed my mind and decided to offer some comments and ideas related to the future of the area. At this writing, the area is confronted with problems and challenges that will profoundly affect its future. Its population loss alone has been severe. When one looks at the population segments lost, the more educated, management demographic, the problem is even more severe. Those who care for the future of this area are concerned for that future.

This book has offered a glimpse of the past that gives some insight into how we arrived at where we are today. It is hoped that this insight also contributes to the challenge of determining where we will be in later years and decades. I offer some basics to consider.

The Basics

There are several principles around which public policy should be shaped as the area moves forward. The first applies to all governments everywhere. And, it applies even more in the Utica-Rome area. Government and politicians do not create jobs. You can't tell this from campaign commercials or by political press releases, but jobs and economies are created by far more important and different players. An economy is the product of large numbers of decisions made by large numbers of people concerning what to produce, buy and sell. Politicians can influence these decisions by increasing or decreasing incentives to produce, work and innovate. On the local level, the primary impact of government, as stated by leaders such as Jack Plumley and Ray Meier is atmospheric. Local government through things like tax policy, zoning process, basic services and the like can offer a business friendly setting for job creation and attraction. Conversely, over taxation and regulation and poor basic services can discourage and force out business. The Utica-Rome area must reform itself to the point of dramatically lowering the cost of doing business. All forms of taxes must be reduced and all regulatory steps affecting business be streamlined. Economic development agencies must have relationships developed under which they can spearhead this needed streamlining.

Second, as silly as this might sound, the area must come to grips with the fact that it is part of New York State and will always be. There will be no downstate-upstate revolution that splits the state into independent ones. Local leaders and citizens in general find solace, pleasure and relief in blaming state government for all of our ills. This amazingly even includes those who represent the area in the state's legislative chambers. The excuse that we are part of a state with the highest taxes and most regulations in the nation and thus can't improve and grow is just that, an excuse that postpones and works against reforming what the area does control.

The better course of action, in fact the only course of action, is to recognize that ugly fact of New York life and strive to create an oasis in the desert. The area should become the state lead in low local taxes, government structural reform, community organization creativity and dedication, local regulatory streamlining and a host of other alterations that will make the area stick out as the best in the state for business development and lifestyle. It would be helpful to look west to the Syracuse area where the Onondaga County Executive is breathing a good deal of fresh air into an Upstate area. That area is more advanced than that of the Utica-Rome area to begin with but faces some of the same problems. We can both learn from and improve some of the approaches being taken a scant hour away. One key problem is the ever increasing cost of local government. The Onondaga County Executive, Joanie Mahoney is breaking impressive new ground in the effort to control cost. Oneida County government is overdue for major reform from top to bottom.

The third is that government can't pick business winners and losers. The track record of government grants and tax breaks to companies to create and grow jobs is abysmal. Shrewd business-men, hucksters and those in between will always hustle the taxpayer bucks out of politicians. Those politicians, all too eager for short term claims and credit to help re-election efforts and to cut ribbons are incapable of saying no to bad business deals. Good companies and good business deals do not have to rely on government money to make them work. The cardinal rule should be is that if a politician would not be willing to invest his own money into a business, he should not invest the taxpayer's money. If such a rule were followed, there would be instant and significant cost savings to the taxpayer and frustration within the community. For each business loss discourages the outlook for the future. The problem is compounded when failure is on the taxpayer's nickel. Keeping these principles in mind, there are a number of steps that can be taken to quickly and effectively reverse the decline of the region.

Is There Hope?

Several years ago, during a lull in our business, my partner and I wrote what we eventually called the *Mohawk Valley Growth Plan, A Blueprint for 21st Century Economic Revival.* My partner, John Spina, and I had earlier joined with a few younger guys to start a new high tech company. John, a trained engineer, had a deep business background and returned at retirement age to the area from northern Virginia. In starting our company, we were motivated to try to make a lot of money and to do it with a new business in the area of our births.

We had a rough business time as most start ups do and often discussed why within the context of the area. On day, we decided to create a much needed area plan which would help spur area wide business growth. We never did do much with it but many of its recommendations merit presentation and consideration. They form the basis for steps that can and should be taken. They involved ways to create high tech jobs through special Rome Labs related projects, steps to lower taxes and consolidate services, creating immigrant business incubators and funding a dramatic, private equity investment apparatus. More important, they represent outside the box thinking which has been in short supply in the area. Since we wrote our plan, signs of change have appeared.

Higher education leaders at place like the SUNY-IT and Hamilton College in particular are breathing new thought into the community. The new SUNY emphasis on cutting edge academic/business approaches has great potential. Groups like the Alexander Hamilton Institute for the Study of Western Civilization are bringing new intellectual life in the form of speakers, projects and student development.

Politically, as a result of national concerns, the tea parties and other types of movements troubled by size of government, spending and taxation are rapidly blossoming.

These groups will not go away and also have the potential to become powerful local, government reform groups. The local taxpayer has finally had enough. Tax revolts have, and are, taking place throughout Central New York. These revolts will ultimately force the structural change that should have taken place decades ago. Both numbers of governmental units and public employees will be reduced. Public funded salaries and benefits will come under scrutiny and control to an extent never before possible. Why? People have run out of money and tolerance to feed the government machine. Serious reform should follow.

With new media forms, the internet, social networking, new immigrant populations as mentioned in the previous section, the message of reform becomes easier to achieve. New forms of knowledge, education and communication are appearing as are new potential leadership groups. None are bound by the constraints of the past. Many could blossom to lead the area into the future.

The most important task confronting the area is one of restoring the balance between the private and public sectors. The private sector represented by business, civic groups, colleges, the media and the taxpayer must seize control of our growth agenda. Old, failed government dominated people, ideas, concepts and programs must be replaced by new, innovative, private initiatives. This realignment will be a daunting job. It will require more people getting involved politically, the marshalling of private monies to create new business investment models and a complete, honest assessment and understanding of the area's problems. We can't sit back and continue to rely on the old clichés used to sugar coat our real deficiencies. The jury is out, at least in this author's mind, on whether or not we are, as a community, up to the challenge.

Part of that challenge must be met by individuals, families and institutions which have little to do with politics or business in a direct sense. It will require an understanding and commitment to "the civic life" defined in a broad sense. That commitment involves things like the responsibility of parenthood, morality based mentoring, instilling a commitment to basic education of our young, including personal responsibility and respect, for an alarming part of our population, particularly centered on our young, have lost the values necessary to develop a healthy community. And, without a healthy community there can be no growth.

The window for advancing the area is still open. It needs to be thrown wide open, and fast. The now stuck window requires the strength of all, citizen, politician, teacher, preacher and business person to open it and let the fresh air in.

The optimism of 40 years ago that inspired the creation of the Assaro movement, built around the theme of capturing, nurturing and promoting the ability and genius of our young and creative adults must be reborn. For it is they who hold the key to the promise of our future.

It is hoped that this book contributes to that rebirth.